Clearing the Way

Thanks for coming
up to me.

Tom Romano

Clearing the Way

Working with Teenage Writers

TOM ROMANO
Edgewood High School
Trenton, Ohio

Heinemann
Portsmouth, NH

Heinemann Educational Books, Inc.
70 Court Street   Portsmouth, NH   03801
Offices and agents throughout the world

Chapter 6 originally appeared in English Journal 75 (September 1986), in a slightly different version under the title "The Process in Process."

Parts of Chapter 7 appeared in English Language Arts Bulletin, Special Issue: Writing, Research, Teaching—Articles from the Ohio Writing Project 23 (Winter/Spring 1982), under the title "Teacher-Student Conferencing: A Way to Writing Improvement."

"Accountability" first appeared in English Journal 75 (March 1986).

The "Rock Fantasia" idea in Chapter 9 first appeared in The Ohio Writing Project Newsletter 3 (April 1983).

The limerick by Kathy Wilham appearing in Chapter 9 was originally published as part of a piece in the "Our Readers Write" column, English Journal 73 (December 1984).

The Walt Whitman writing prompt appearing in Chapter 10 was originally published in "Of Whitman and Friend," English Journal 73 (December 1984).

Library of Congress Cataloging-in-Publication Data

Romano, Tom.
  Clearing the way.

  Includes bibliographies and index.
    1. English language—Study and teaching (Secondary)—United States.   2. English language—United States—Composition and exercises.   I. Title.
  LB1631.R59   1987   428'.007'12   86-29558
  ISBN 0-435-08439-9

Front-cover photo by James Whitney.
Back-cover photo by Rebecca Butts.
Designed by Wladislaw Finne.
Printed in the United States of America.

10 9 8 7 6 5 4 3 2

The hard, joyous work that was the writing of this book is dedicated to three women:

My daughter, Mariana, who began teaching me to see soon after she started talking.

My wife, Kathy, who has survived much, grown strong, and remained loving.

My mother, Mae, who won an essay contest in 1930 when she was fifteen. She had written about pottery making, a subject her family knew well. When asked to read her essay, she did and grew increasingly pale and terrified as she stood before her classmates on that, the last day she ever attended school.

A writer is a writer regardless of degrees.

Donald Graves,
responding in a student's journal

Contents

Students have voices, things to say uniquely and powerfully if they are permitted free rein. The teacher's job is to set up an atmosphere in which students feel safe to cut loose with their language, to set words down boldly.

Communicating is not the only job that language can do. No better tool exists for thinking new things and learning new concepts. Through writing, students can use their personal language to think and learn in all classrooms, in every discipline.

An ever-renewed knowledge of writing from the experience of doing it leads to deep understanding and compassionate teaching. Teachers are warmly invited to engage in the satisfying act of writing, to become frequent practitioners of the craft they teach.

ix

Acknowledgments

These people, irreplaceable:

Don Graves, Jane Hansen, Lorri Neilsen, and Ruth Hubbard, a writing group par excellence.

The thousands of Edgewood High School students whose words have instructed and delighted me.

The children and teachers, particularly Jan Roberts, of Mast Way School in Lee, New Hampshire, who passed on to me warmth and wisdom during the year I spent in the Mast Way Reading/Writing Research Project (1983–85).

Don Graves, who knew this book could be written before I did, and said so to his editor.

Philippa Stratton, editor-in-chief of Heinemann, who buoyed me throughout the writing.

Donna Bouvier, my production editor at Heinemann, whose expert eye and gentle queries helped me make a better book.

Steve Zemelman, whose detailed and upbeat critique of my book prospectus I referred to often for guidance and spirit boosts in the early going.

Nancie Atwell, who knows how to cut to the bone and still keep a writer writing, and who can talk to someone on the telephone for five minutes and have him walking a good foot off the floor.

Mary Chris Reese, of Morse High School, Bath, Maine, whose response to my trial chapters convinced me I could reach teachers.

Carolyn Smith and John Gaughan, friends and fellow English teachers who read early drafts of most of the chapters and then wrote and told how the words hit them.

Arlene Silberman, a writer from New York City who read part of my manuscript and then gave me phone calls and notes of support and cheer.

Linda Rief of Oyster River Middle School in Durham, New Hampshire, who read all my writing, responded, and made me think, and think again.

Don Murray, that consummate wordsmith, excellent manuscript reader, and tireless supporter of writers; and Minnie Mae Murray, who deals in baked delectables and straight talk.

Ken Macrorie, who said in his books so well so long ago so many things I felt in my bones.

Stephen Tchudi, editor of *English Journal*, 1973–80, who wrote me a kind and helpful rejection letter, then later published a piece of mine.

Alleen Pace Nilsen and Ken Donelson, editors of *English Journal*, 1980–87, who have published much of what I've sent them.

My department head, Phyllis Neumann; principal, Gene Smith; past superintendent, Roger Compton; and present superintendent, Bill Bishop, who continually cleared the way for me so that I might try and do and grow.

Milton White, author of *A Yale Man*; professor emeritus of Miami University; and, quite simply, a teacher without peer.

Ohio Writing Project directors Mary Fuller and Max Morenberg and assistant director Janet Ziegler, who continue to have an unsurpassed positive influence on the teaching of writing in Ohio.

Nancy, my sister, a believer for years.

Mark Hayes, who gave me jazz, friendship, and some of the best words.

And Kathy—wife, friend, exceptional nurse—who gives me the mental, physical, and emotional room to write. Thank you.

Note to the Reader

My book contains over thirty examples of student writing. Some of them were dashed off in minutes; some were labored over by the authors; some were submitted to editors who cleaned them up and published them in a school creative-arts anthology.

I give you the student writing here in whatever stage it finally reached. The pieces often contain errors of writing etiquette. I let them stand, not out of disrespect for the writers, but out of respect for error and the part it plays in the process of writing.

Human beings are usually messy when they create. And the experience of one writer is never identical to the experience of another. People differ in their development, skills, priorities, and focus. We writing teachers need to acknowledge these differences and learn to look through the messiness to the matter of each student's writing. So the errors stand.

Whenever possible, I have secured permission from the students to publish their writing.

As I wrote this book, I kept in mind my audience—hungry secondary-school English teachers. I am one myself—always something gnawing at me, always looking to meet my needs as an English teacher, to satisfy my hunger. I find what I need, but soon I am looking for more. Good teachers rarely remain satisfied long. They are ever rummaging around.

Rummage in my book and you will find ideas you can use immediately, attitudes that may alter how you work with students, and theory that makes sense. You will also find a wide cast of characters and a great many stories. They are the heart of my book. I have learned from all of them and hope you will too.

The book is born out of my own struggles to write well and fourteen years of working hard with teenage writers. Both the writing and the working have been worth it. They are fine passions.

Cutting Loose

I had never seen my thirteen-year-old daughter display such uncharacteristic behavior. Hands folded upon her lap, she sat stiffly in a high-backed chair. Her riotous, curly blonde hair was pulled back in a tight bun. Her lips were unsmiling, her cheeks pale, her eyes expressionless. Occasionally, she blinked. That and one long, notable yawn were her only movements.

The most uncharacteristic detail of all, and the most disturbing, involved her voice. It was silent.

For an instant, however, I believed she was about to dramatically break her silence and inactivity. Life suddenly flickered into her eyes; she appeared desperate to end both the demure behavior and atypical silence by launching into one of her brash, exuberant monologs. But the instant passed. The life faded from her eyes; the desperation turned to resignation. She ended as she had begun—quiet, polite, self-effacing, indistinguishable from anybody else.

See for yourself:

> I have always wanted to visit Italy. Much of my family is from Italy. I have been told stories, and have seen pictures of how beautiful Italy is. I would like to go to the small town of Naples, where my grandfather was born. I also love Italian food! I'm sure I'd get enough there! These are some reasons I would like to visit Italy.

I saw this glimpse of my daughter at the beginning of summer, her eighth-grade year just completed. The date on the paper indicated that she had written this piece in early November. It lay in her writing folder, clipped to a dozen similarly constructed paragraphs. I still couldn't believe, didn't want to believe, that the personality revealed in the writing was my daughter's. This couldn't be the same blood of my blood who, in the years prior to her formal education, had taught me how to see anew through her richly metaphorical view of the world. This couldn't be the curious girl I bantered with about books and films and current events. This couldn't be the opinionated, argumentative, brand-new teenager I was starting to tangle with about complex social issues as well as how much makeup was too much. This couldn't be Mariana.

But it was. The subject matter gave her away. The writing was undeniably hers. My father had indeed been born in a dusty village near Naples in 1905, and our family had been planning a trip to Italy for some time. Furthermore (and this was the irrefutable evidence), Mariana did love Italian food enough to stir an exclamatory flicker of life in that listless, prim little paragraph.

I decided to try an experiment on that summer day. I made no comments about the paragraphs I'd read from her writing folder. Instead, I asked her if she would do a piece of nonstop, focused freewriting the next morning on a topic I would write on a slip of paper and seal in an envelope. She agreed. When she arose the next morning, this is what she found in the envelope:

So, Mariana, you want to go to Italy?
I bet. A likely story.
But if you really do want to go to Italy then convince me of it with words on paper.
Time yourself—really. Fifteen or twenty minutes should do it.
Talk straight and give me the specifics.

Papa

When I returned home later that day, I found an envelope addressed to me with this inside:

Yes, I want to go to Italy. this should be easy!

My family is from Italy, I would like to see where Grandpa and family is from. Liz told me that she loved it when she went, some parts are beautiful but the only proplem is the people don't brush their teeth! (yuk!) I bet the dentists could make alot of money!

You can't forget that I did my country report on Italy. I read about the mountains and the different places there are.

I also think any place but the U. S. would be fun to explore, see and hear new things. Have an adventure (hopefully not like the Clipper Ship Adventure!)

The food! Oh, real, authentic Italian food! Squid! Spagehtti, sauce, clams! Yum! We'll just find out how close America's Italian" is to the real thing!

There are many places to see, Flourence, Venice with the water, Moddona Glace where Grandpa was born, Naples, Rome! So many new things to explore.

I've always been proud of my Italian heritage so it would be great to see, hear, explore, and taste.

Now whats this likely story bussiness? Have I convinced you? How about you convincing me? Maybe your wanting to go to Italy is a likely story also, eh?

Now this was more like my daughter, a high-spirited teenager full of facts, opinions, hearsay, prejudices, and passions, a critic keyed to irony and fond of turning the questioning upon her inquisitor. How could she contain such diverse personalities? The voice, the information, and the structure of the two pieces were so strikingly different I simply had to interview her about them. I read both pieces aloud to her, then asked, "Did you remember you had done this first, shorter version back in November?"

"Nope."

"How did this first one come about?"

"It was assigned that we had to write about a place we always wanted to visit."

"You got to choose, huh?"

"Yeah," she said, "and you had to have a topic sentence, three supporting details, and a concluding sentence."

"How come?"

"'Cause that's what we had to do."

"Did you have any other rules to follow, any form?"

"Not really. Just that we had to have a topic sentence and write about a place we always wanted to visit."

"How do you explain the difference in the two pieces?"

"What do you mean?"

"Well," I said, "I think the one you wrote this morning is far more effective. It's an honest, lively piece of writing. People would much rather read it than . . ."

"That was free and the other was a form."

"What form?"

"Topic sentence, supporting details, and concluding sentence."

"You have all those things in the one you wrote this morning, too," I said. "Topic sentence: 'Yes, I want to visit Italy.'"

"Not the same," said Mariana impatiently.

"You know, I'll bet your teacher would have been much happier with the kind of writing you did this morning. I mean, it really sounds like there's somebody behind the words."

"Well, she wanted what I gave her."

"How do you know?"

"I got it back with a check on it. It was *O—K!*"

I'd have been in danger of getting slashed if my daughter's tone became much sharper. It was telling me, "Back off, Buddy, or this could get ugly." I decided to risk a cut.

"What do you think you learned about writing this year?"

Mariana was silent; I waited.

"How to do paragraphs," she said finally.

"When do you think you'll use that?"

"I don't know . . . well, for my term papers."

"Term papers?"

"Yeah, the teacher said that next year when we get in high school, we'd write a lot of term papers."

"So on term papers you'll write like this," I said, pointing to the dead November paragraph, "as opposed to writing like you did this morning?"

"I don't know!" Mariana exploded. "The teacher kept telling us we have to learn this this year! 'We have to teach you how to do a proper paragraph—the topic sentence, the supporting details, and the concluding sentence.'"

Our interview ended there. Her teachers could be well-satisfied, I reflected. My daughter had learned what had been emphasized. I was certain that she could pick out "proper" paragraph form on any objective test in the land. I was also certain that she would probably continue to write a great many dismally proper paragraphs in school because that is what she knew teachers wanted. Some teachers, no doubt, do want such lifeless writing. In fact, they actively solicit it. Instead of celebrating each student's unique personality, particular way of seeing, and personal brand of English, these teachers neglect them in favor of stressing artificial writing forms and easy-to-follow recipes—pick a subject, any subject, exercise all the freedom you want, but write *this* way, use *this* form.

Such regimentation and squelching of variety shouldn't surprise anybody. Our culture is full of it. We vote for only two presidential candidates. Much of the music on popular radio sounds the same. Fast-food restaurants serve prepackaged, identical sandwiches. And many English teachers, in their genuinely conscientious efforts to teach students how to write— how to write *properly*—devise all kinds of schemes and methods that succeed in stripping writing of personality, in promoting a pretentious, impersonal point of view, and in censoring all but a safe, near-mechanical use of our living language. Too often, writing instruction is designed not to set students free, but to shackle them, whip them into line, restrict their movement, make each like the other.

Here's one set of manacles clamped upon students before they begin self-expression:

CHARACTERIZATION

This composition assignment is to be a characterization of one of your friends. The format is to be as follows:

1. In the topic sentence, introduce your friend and use three adjectives to describe him/her.
2. Sentences 2 and 3 give examples of the first adjective.
3. Sentences 4 and 5 give examples of the second adjective.
4. Sentences 6 and 7 give examples of the third adjective.
5. Sentence 8 restates the topic sentence, using synonyms for each of the three adjectives.

Note: This is not necessarily a 3–8 composition. You

may use more than two examples for any of the three
adjectives.

6. The manuscript form is to be as follows:
    A. The heading should consist of three lines (Name,
       Date, and Characterization) and should appear in
       the upper right-hand corner.
    B. Write in blue or black ink only.
    C. Write on every other line.
    D. Observe both margins.
    E. Begin the composition on the second line of the
       paper.
7. Check to make sure you have used varied sentence
   openers.
8. Double-check to be sure you have followed all of
   these directions.

I was relieved to learn that this composition wasn't necessarily
of the 3–8 variety. I don't know what a 3–8 composition is,
and I don't want to know. The assignment alone is horror
enough.

Although such abuses in the teaching of writing exist, I
still believe that the state of writing instruction in secondary
schools is not totally bleak—that it is, in fact, on the upswing.
At presentations and conferences I've met many good teachers
of writing, teachers who themselves write and whose goal is
to help young writers grow. I am confident that during the
rest of her public schooling, my daughter will come under
the guidance of at least one or two of these teachers. They
know that for students to write well, something must take
place of far more significance than the learning of patterns
and formulas. Young writers must be cut loose. They must
write frequently in high-speed chases after meaning, adventures
that will take various routes, each different from the previous
one.

When students hand in writing, I don't want their foremost
concern to be whether punctuation and spelling are correct,
or whether they have properly followed a form they've been
taught. Instead, I want them eager to learn how well their
words worked. I want *what* they have to say to be of primary
importance to them and to those who are following and nur-
turing their growth as writers.

My daughter's first, perfunctory "Why I want to visit Italy" piece is the result of form taking primacy over meaning. Mariana knew this. She jumped through the hoop, performed the ritual, and, like an assembly-line worker, collected her check. Sadly, in this assignment she saw no opportunity to explore a subject that had personal importance to her. She had learned that having a topic sentence, three supporting details, and a concluding sentence was more important than anything else, including her meaning, her thinking, and her own voice—in short, those things that make her human.

C. H. Knoblauch and Lil Brannon write that instruction that emphasizes the form and correctness of writing over meaning "is like having to learn table manners before getting a chance to eat" (1984, 47). This pointed comparison sparks another one in my mind, one that views the metaphor of food from a different angle, casting the young writer as chef. In my daughter's case I argue that her learned preoccupation with the form of the meal prevented her from preparing anything more than meager fare for her reader.

In those dozen topic-sentence paragraphs moldering in her folder, my daughter's voice was as bland as the marinara sauce served in second-rate restaurants. Those innocuous concoctions offend few but appeal to none. Without a distinctive voice, no writer will produce distinctive writing. Donald Graves has written that voice is "the dynamo of the writing process" (1983, 31). Voice generates writing. If this is so, then information is the electricity for that dynamo, and a positive self-concept flips the power switch and keeps that dynamo generating. As a writer loses self-consciousness, the voice becomes bolder; as confidence increases, the voice becomes distinctive.

In any writing class, then, the first and constant order of business is to enable all students to establish and develop their individual voices. Teachers must cut them loose the first day. Let them write in any form they choose. But make sure they write and sustain that writing long enough to rev up their voices. Ken Macrorie (1976) and Peter Elbow (1973) call such activity "freewriting." Donald Murray (1983) has called it "following a line of language."

Call it whatever you like. Just be sure to cut students loose. Let them write rapidly and frequently for a set amount of time—say, ten minutes in the beginning of a course—without regard to error, expectation, or self. Let them and you find out what they sound like when they know their words will not be marked wrong, when adhering to a particular form is not the prime requirement, when failure is an impossibility.

Such free or nonstop writing should be a staple in every English class. Its objective, its goal, is the development of fluency and self-confidence—the parents of voice. Plenty of honest language production—fluency—is the sole criterion for successful freewriting. Quality of language production is not. But even so, frequent engagement in rapid writing will improve the quality of writing.

I am always amazed by those who climb to a high board, pause briefly, and then execute a flawless dive. And I am likewise amazed by those who, in a short time and with virtually no revision, produce a compelling piece of writing. We must always remember, however, that such perfection is achieved through thousands of practice dives, through plenty of real writing experience. The key to helping our student writers grow is to keep them writing.

In John Irving's novel *The Hotel New Hampshire*, Lilly, the dwarfish sister and dedicated writer of the family, is intent upon improving her writing skills, upon learning to produce high-quality prose. She writes constantly. Family members sometimes knock on her locked door and ask, "What are you doing, Lilly?" She always replies, "Trying to grow" (1981, 264). And she does grow, albeit not physically. Lilly grows into a good writer.

As writing teachers, we rarely need to be severe critics. It is the least of our roles. Our foremost role is head of maintenance. We need to switch on our students' dynamos and keep them in good running order. And we need to see that our students become adept at switching on their own dynamos, at confidently letting their voices move across the page. The more writing becomes second nature to students, the greater the likelihood that they will generate powerful written language.

Practice, frequent doing, is what will enable writing to become natural to students. That isn't surprising. The Zen idea of daily doing makes any activity as effortless as breathing. In my attempt to keep physically fit, for example, I swim, usually a mile and a quarter each time I enter the pool. I couldn't begin to swim that far if I had to concentrate on executing each stroke, each breath, each flip turn. Those must become automatic so that I can get into my swimming rhythm.

So it is with writing. Most students are not used to it. Or if they are used to writing, it's a kind of trivial pursuit in which they are penalized if they somehow produce it improperly.

And that is precisely why the bulk of the writing done in school should be done with no formal attention paid to errors of grammar, style, spelling, or usage—not that teachers should never attend to teaching students the standard conventions of writing. They should, but only in the final stage of completing a piece. And, of course, I don't mean to imply that students should flout the conventions of writing. What I mean is that the aspects of writing that should be emphasized in schools are those that are most important: the pursuit of meaning and the development of each student's particular way of speaking with words on paper—voice.

In *A Vulnerable Teacher*, Ken Macrorie writes, "I now see that a teacher must quickly arrange things so the students reveal themselves at their best" (1974, 100). The implementation of nonstop writing in classrooms can do this. If teachers are willing to cut students loose by letting them write from the very first day, if they are willing to accept their students' dialects, idiolects, and developing understanding of written language conventions, students will quickly learn that they need not fear and loathe paper and pen. They will readily take up the tools of a writer and produce writing of personal importance. From this point, they may begin learning more about the craft of writing.

The students that trouble me most are those tough, silent ones we all long to reach. In classrooms they are nearly mute. They neither speak nor write much at all. One reason for their silence, I think, is because they believe no one—particularly no adult—is interested in what they have to say. They are like Randall Jarrell's protagonist in *The Bat-Poet*, who came to understand that "The trouble isn't making poems, the trouble's finding somebody that will listen to them" (1963, 15). A teacher, any teacher, but especially a language-arts teacher, is in an excellent position to show students that someone is interested in what they have to say, that there are adults who care about more than the propriety of their language and the correctness of writing forms.

A teacher is crucial to the success or failure of a writing class. She is a temporary catalyst, stirring students to life in their writing often enough for them to experience the power of their words. The teacher must demonstrate to students that nothing is binding them. They are free to say what they like in the ways that are most natural to them, that *become* most natural to them. (We must remember, after all, that students will grow and change as writers.) Once students trust that they are truly cut loose, they will soon write honestly and with full voices. It becomes habit.

Early in my teaching career I was influenced by *Hooked on Books* (1966), Daniel Fader and Elton McNeil's excellent book, which liberated many a language-arts classroom. In my junior–senior level class, condescendingly titled Basic Skills, I immediately set up a reading and writing program adapted from the one Fader and McNeil described. As they recommended, I had students keep journals. I began keeping one myself. I told the students that journal writing would account for one-fifth of their total course grade. The journals were theirs; they could say anything they liked in them. I would not mark them. I would not even read them, unless they asked me to. Grades for journal writing would be earned by the quantity of writing produced. I would collect the journals each week and thumb through them to determine how much they had written. Three pages per week earned a C, four a B, and five an A.

"What if we write more than five pages?" asked one ambitious student.

"That," I said with a magnanimous wave of my hand, "will earn you an A+."

After a few weeks, most of the students were writing journals, although a small number of them, mainly boys, were not writing at all. I made a new rule. The writing of weekly journals, I told them, was so important that in order to pass the class each student must also pass journal writing. That got everyone moving.

Except Scott. A reluctant attender of school, an inmate of what seemed to him a repressive and useless institution, Scott counted the days until he would at last be sprung. He was a loner who wore a perpetual day or two's growth of beard. An imposing presence, he stood six feet one and weighed 190 pounds, a superb combination of bone, muscle, and skepticism. For the first six weeks of school he sat scowling from the back of the room at the desk closest to the door. We gradually came to respect each other. I was straight with him, and courteous. He did what he had to do in order to pass.

But writing in a journal was not Scott's cup of tea, or, more appropriately, stein of beer. He handed in the journal irregularly. Near the end of the course, when the last journal was due, he had written so infrequently that he needed a five-page entry, a solid A, to avoid failing. My surefire plan for closing loopholes had put us both in a corner. I asked Scott to come up to my desk so that I might tell him of his situation and show him the goods in the grade book.

Scott stood beside me, gazing intently, tracing with a motor-oil–stained forefinger the lineup of zeros that followed his name.

"You gotta write one more, Scott, so you can pass the course."

He frowned severely, straightened his frame, borrowed a pencil from the cupful on my desk, and strode back to his seat. Opening his journal, he dug in. For twenty-five minutes he never looked up, just kept bent to the page writing, his jaw set firmly. He looked determined, ready to accept a hard left hook so he could deliver his own powerful right cross to the chin.

At the beginning of the course when I told students I would not read their journals, I meant it. And I had kept my word. But when the bell rang and Scott walked to the front of the room, dropped the fearsomely blunted pencil into the cup, and plopped his journal atop the stack on my desk, I knew I was going to breach the faith, break the promise, betray my word—just this once.

> This is the stupidest damn thing in Edgewood school. If I thought I had to have a diary like a 14 year old girl I'd have one. But I'm a 17 year old guy who doesn't give a damn about no journal. Why fail a person just because he can't sit around and write. Edgewood is a bunch of Bull Shit. Either that or High School Education in Ohio needs someone that isn't a god damn College Graduate to make some changes. I have my own life and mind. I don't need no damn idiots telling me I need to write my thoughts. Thats stupid. If a shrink read this he'd say "Look, he's proving how young people need to

write their feelings or tell them to someone. To that I
say bull shit. I don't talk with my parents and I don't
keep know god damn journal and I'm sane as hell. They
say read a journal from two years ago and see how your
feelings have changed. I don't give a big shit. I only
care about now and maybe tomorrow. I'll think about
yesterday when I'm some old fat assed man, retired, sitting on my front porch smoking a pipe. People who
worry about stuff like journals and feelings and their
pasts are wasting their time. they spend so much time
worrying about what they've done they burn out and
end up not doing anything.

If you get into writing journals and watching plays
and reading Shakespere, go do it and all the power to
you, but leave me the hell out of it. I don't want no
part of it. I like getting crazy on weekends and raising
hell wherever I go. I might end up in the gutter but at
least I won't be surrounded by books and journals, reading about what I did 20 years ago.

School would be easy if they taught you what you
need to know and didn't force stupid shit down your
throat. To hell with everyone of these school bastards.
The only reason I'm not 18 is because I wasn't born
early enough. My mom and dad know it and I let everyone else that crosses me know it too. I do what I want.
If I didn't like Mr. Romano I would have told him to
go to hell when he told me to write this. and when I get
this back I'll rip it up and throw it away. To hell with
saving it for the future. To hell with people who want
me to do it. I'm still mad as hell. The only thing I got
out of writing this is a sore hand. So how do ya like
that for education. I got to write to the bottom line of
this paper for sure. So my last line is—Go straight to
hell Edgewood Cougars.

Scott Shuler, junior

Scott had cut loose. And I shivered in the excitement that
comes with finishing a powerful piece of writing. He showed
what he, an average teenager, was capable of writing when
hotly pursuing a topic without regard to form or the amenities
of writing. Although he was polite enough to play the game

and deliver us both from the absurd corner I'd put us into, Scott refused to be bullied. The staunch independence and fierce individuality present in his writing was an inherent part of his personality. But those traits had rarely asserted themselves in the other writing he'd done. On this occasion, his boiling anger had propelled him to fluency and an unmistakable voice— the goals of journal writing. In fact, Scott had ridden voice and fluency to create the kind of writing that teachers yearn for their students to generate. The entry was direct, strong-stanced, compelling, and chock full of connected assertions.

It contained:

• Vivid imagery ("some old fat assed man, retired, sitting on my front porch smoking a pipe").

• Deadpan humor ("The only reason I'm not 18 is because I wasn't born early enough").

• Parallel structure and strong rhythm ("If you get into writing journals and watching plays and reading Shakespere, go do it and all the power to you, but leave me the hell out of it").

• Effective use of other voices ("If a shrink read this he'd say "Look, he's proving how young people need to write their feelings or tell them to someone").

• Pointed sense of irony ("The only thing I got out of writing this is a sore hand. So how do ya like that for education").

• A startling, definitive close ("Go straight to hell Edgewood Cougars").

• All in a one-shot, rapidly written, unrevised piece of freewriting.

Scott's journal entry was a striking illustration of Ken Macrorie's assertion "When a person is bearing down hard as he can to tell truths, great things happen. His sentences pick up rhythms. He slides into a style that fits his subject. One true, telling detail leads to another" (1974, 146).

Although the main goal of journal writing, of any kind of freewriting, is not the production of high-quality prose, it often happens. When cut loose from premature concerns about correctness and proper forms, when freed to use the language they've been able to write for years, teenagers will strike phrases, lines, paragraphs, and sometimes whole pages that are nothing short of good writing.

Scott's writing during that last week of school is the best example I've seen of that. And I wasn't supposed to read it. Students wrote thousands of journal entries in those Basic Skills classes. Even though I read but few of them (and always thereafter, be assured, only at a student's request), I've no doubt that those teenage writers produced strong writing frequently. My faith is not blind. It comes from the many free-writings my students have done that I have read. In one set of twenty-five, it is not difficult to fill a page with excerpts of effective prose. The more practice students get with free-writing, the more confident their voices become. Confident voices begin producing good passages frequently.

It seems clear that what we must strive to achieve with our writing students is the same thing that American poet Walt Whitman was attuned to in 1855 when he published *Leaves of Grass*. He knew the power of the individual, the immense vitality embodied in a robust and active *I*, one who would, in Whitman's words, "permit to speak at every hazard, / Nature without check with original energy" (27).

We English teachers sometimes seem surrounded by madness—demands for competency-based tests of composing ability, minimum standards, ludicrous quantitative measures of writing skill, a vain clamor for objectivity in assessing the inherently idiosyncratic, subjective act of writing. Amid this madness we too easily lose sight of our primary goal. We must encourage, beckon, urge, even incite every one of our students to write— not occasionally and not in proper paragraphs or five-paragraph essays or some other artificial rhetorical mode, but often, and in their individual voices, each cut loose, each growing, changing, and maturing by the very act of writing, and "each," to quote Whitman again, "singing what belongs to him or her and to none else" (14).

REFERENCES

Elbow, Peter. 1973. *Writing Without Teachers*. New York: Oxford University Press.

Fader, Daniel N., and McNeil, Elton B. 1966. *Hooked on Books: Program & Proof*. New York: Berkley Medallion Books.

Graves, Donald H. 1983. *Writing: Teachers & Children at Work*. Portsmouth, NH: Heinemann.

Irving, John. 1981. *The Hotel New Hampshire*. New York: E. P. Dutton.

Jarrell, Randall. 1963. Pictures by Maurice Sendak. *The Bat-Poet*. New York: Collier Books, a division of Macmillan Publishing Co.

Knoblauch, C. H., and Brannon, Lil. 1984. *Rhetorical Traditions and the Teaching of Writing*. Upper Montclair, NJ: Boynton/Cook.

Macrorie, Ken. 1974. *A Vulnerable Teacher*. Rochelle Park, NJ: Hayden Book Co.

———. 1976. *Writing to Be Read*. 2d rev. ed. Rochelle Park, NJ: Hayden Book Co.

Murray, Donald. 1983. Keynote address at the Second Miami University Conference on Sentence Combining and the Teaching of Writing in Oxford, OH, October 1983. Later published as "Writing Badly to Write Well: Searching for the Instructive Line." In *Sentence Combining: A Rhetorical Perspective*, edited by Donald A. Daiker, Andrew Kerek, and Max Morenberg. Carbondale, IL: Southern Illinois University Press, 1985.

Whitman, Walt. 1981. "Song of Myself" and "I Hear America Singing." In *Leaves of Grass*. Franklin Center, PA: The Franklin Library. (Originally published in 1855.)

Using Writing

I sit on the sharing rug with twenty third graders and their teacher, Jan Roberts, of Mast Way School in Lee, New Hampshire. As part of Donald Graves and Jane Hansen's research team at the University of New Hampshire, I am gathering data on children's development as readers and writers. I've been visiting this classroom daily for more than three months. This day in our sharing circle Eddie sits upon the lone chair—the author's chair. He has just finished reading aloud his piece about fishing. Eddie calls upon the seven children who have their hands raised, and each, in turn, comments and asks questions about his writing.

Eddie smiles, a fat cat in literacy learning. He relishes being in charge, hearing his words responded to, and divulging additional information about fishing. Eddie calls upon Melissa.

She shifts her legs so that she is sitting on one of her sneakers. She bends her blond head forward, looking at Eddie's feet rather than his contented smile. She speaks hesitantly: "Did you ever notice . . . or, well . . . realize anything while you were writing?"

"No," says Eddie, too quickly. He is puzzled by Melissa's inquiry. Many of the other children are too.

"Melissa," I say, "has that happened to you? Have you realized something while you were actually writing?"

"Yes," she answers softly. She seems embarrassed to reveal this. "Once when I was writing about an Encyclopedia Brown book, I realized one of the clues while I was writing."

"How does that happen?" I ask. "How do you realize something at the same time you're writing?"

"I just do," says Melissa. "Kaboom! And it's there."

On that dreary, cold New Hampshire morning, Melissa described the aspect of writing that comes closest to magic. We write and soon find ourselves putting down facts we didn't know were in our heads. We write and explain something lucidly that had been only a foggy notion. We write and create examples that illustrate our generalizations. We write and suddenly "realize" or "notice" things.

This seemingly magical aspect of writing is a "Now you *don't* see it, now you *do*" proposition. And the reason it works has a great deal to do with fluency. We—teachers, students, writers all—must be willing and able to put down words boldly with the sole purpose of getting at thinking, at personal truth. Fluency in writing sets the stage for surprises. That's why it is crucial for students to believe their written words are for more than mere correcting. And that's why we must make a priority of helping students develop confidence in putting words on paper. Once fluent, students can experience the magic, make discoveries, know the "kaboom." Peter Elbow explains how the apparent magic works:

> Once you get yourself writing in an exploratory but uncensored fashion, the ongoing string of language and syntax itself becomes a lively and surprising force for generation. Words call up words, ideas call up more ideas. A momentum of language and thinking develops and one learns to nurture it by keeping the pen moving. (1983, 39)

Even with Elbow's helpful explanation, an element of magic remains. Words and ideas call up more words and ideas. Writing is a continual process of linguistic invocation, involving just enough mystery to excite us. We never can be entirely sure what words and ideas will be summoned, and we often do not perceive where they are taking us until we have arrived.

Magicians, of course, don't work without tools. They may use wands or rings, top hats or black boxes. Writers also use a special tool, one far more versatile than any wand or ring, one they have been working comfortably with and refining for years. The tool is language. It is personal and distinct. Each writer's language, each student's language, has the owner's marks all over it—fingerprints of the intellect and environment, idiosyncrasies of vocabulary, grammar, and dialect, even the sound of a particular voice. Like a pair of shoes broken in for good walking, the writer's language fits only one. It would feel awkward and ill-fitting on another.

In addition to being highly individual, each student's language is capable of creating, reinforcing, and solidifying personal knowledge. In fact, there's nothing like the intense thinking that goes on when we use language deliberately in writing. As Tom Newkirk says, "It may be *the* major instrument" for learning (1986, 3).

And yet in classroom after classroom students do little writing of consequence. Instead, they listen—maybe. Or, when they do write, as Arthur Applebee discovered in his 1981 study of the writing in American secondary schools, students merely take notes, fill in blanks, or write brief answers of one or two lines. Rarely do teachers ask students to turn their language, with all its potential for magic, to the subject under study. Rarely do teachers ask students to take what is most familiar to them and use it to understand what is unfamiliar.

This is lamentable. Teachers in every discipline must come to realize that writing is not merely a means of communicating messages. They must understand "that writing is basic to thinking about, and learning knowledge in all fields. . . ." (Fulwiler 1983, 224).

WRITING TO CREATE AND EXPLORE THINKING

In the film communication classes I teach, my students write after just about every film we see, and we see more than thirty during a semester. Sometimes I ask students to write about certain techniques, like camera angles or lighting. But usually I just ask them to write rapidly for five to ten minutes, responding specifically to the images and sound, trying hard to make sense. My purpose is to engage them in deep, sustained thinking. Writing compels them to do that.

One film we see is *Time Piece* by Jim Henson of Muppet fame. It is offbeat, funny, and loaded with pointed surprises created by editing. Henson himself plays the central character, who is trapped by his mundane job, ho-hum sex life, need to make money, and bland middle-class life-style. We see him move through a day in scenes and sequences cut to various monotonously rhythmic sound effects that are interrupted occasionally by raucous bursts from a jazz drummer. I show *Time Piece* when we are studying editing, particularly unconventional shot juxtaposition. The film is perfect for that. Henson cuts together shots that have nothing and everything to do with each other. For example, at one point we see this sequence:

Medium shot—Henson and wife being seated at a table in a nightclub.

Close-up—Henson intently watching stage.

Medium shot—silhouetted figure of stripper, moving seductively.

Close-up—a wide-eyed Henson, gulping.

Close-up—a dog, panting.

The final, unconventional cutaway to the dog surprises the students into understanding laughter. The images of gulping man and panting dog each carries a distinct meaning. But cut together in a certain context, the two images generate what Russian pioneer filmmaker Sergei Eisenstein called a "third meaning" (Kuhns and Stanley 1969). *Time Piece* contains many unconventional shot juxtapositions; and, happily, it is like nothing the students have ever seen in their thousands of hours watching television.

After seeing *Time Piece*, one eleventh-grade boy wrote:

> I think the film was about things that are happening
> in society. One thing I didn't understand (one of the
> many) was why did the man keep saying "help." I
> didn't really understand the movie all that well.

Half-thoughts, vagueness, and capitulation. Sometimes that happens. What bothers me about this writing, though, is that the student did not faithfully do as I'd asked. He did not use the entire allotted time to pursue with language his puzzlements. He wrote briefly. Ironically, he mentions one of the key elements in the film: the protagonist's feeble and futile cries for help. But instead of thinking specifically about those instances, he quit writing. The magic never had a chance to work. He possessed little faith. And, as Jacques Cousteau or innovative

jazz trumpeter-composer Miles Davis would tell you, faith is
a must when seeking discoveries. The writer must keep writing,
even when he fears he is producing little of value, as the
following eleventh-grade boy did:

> I saw a bunch of nonsense. I think this guy was flip-
> ping out. The film sort of followed him thru a day. He
> went to work, came home and ate supper, and then he
> and his wife went out. As the day went along I guess he
> imagined himself as a wild-animalistic type person. Like
> when he was on his way home thru the woods he turned
> into Tarzan. Sometimes he was shown in real ragged
> clothes. He had sex on his mind alot. The action went
> right along with the beat of the music.
> I think he felt his life was a big rat race going down
> the toilet because every so often he asked for help.

Kaboom! He hadn't seen a bunch of nonsense after all, and
his language let him know it. I look at his first condemnatory,
frustrated line and marvel at how the student got himself to
that last line, which states a theme of the film. He got there,
of course, through following language, through writing, "the
most disciplined form of thinking" (Murray 1984, 4).

Doug, one of my American Literature students who kept
a response journal on his reading, explains this process of
using language to discover thought: "You can think more and
understand when you write. You can write ideas you think
are important and questions that you don't understand. Also,
if you write, your questions may be answered if you ramble
on for awhile."

Although usually inappropriate for pieces of writing to be
delivered to an audience, "rambling on for awhile" is eminently
appropriate for discovery writing. In fact, this kind of writing
isn't really meant for an audience. A teacher's judgment of
it is not only unnecessary, but quite possibly detrimental to
further attempts at exploratory writing. The writing is only
secondarily for the teacher; it is primarily for the student—
it is her language, her thinking, her learning. Watch this
eleventh-grade girl ramble over the facts of *Time Piece*:

> There was a man in the hospital getting his heartbeat
> checked, and they used different sounds to represent

things, like when his eyes blinked it was the sound of a
camera. When he walked, he walked to the beat of
drums. He thought about different things like sex. It
also showed when he was in the dollar bill and said help
that maybe he had money troubles. When he ate he
went back in time with his wife eating like they did in
earlier times. When he shot the Mona Lisa they arrested
him and took him to prison. Then he escaped and ran
away and flew off. They sent rockets and bombs at him
and he said help.

Everything was with a beat to the music, maybe his
life was based on time.

All students who faithfully write for the allotted time do
not lead themselves to such succinct statements of theme. But
all of them think; no one remains passive while engaged in
such productive written rambling. In advocating students
keeping learning journals in content areas throughout the curriculum, Toby Fulwiler points out that "every time students
write entries they are individualizing their instruction; writing
silently—even for five minutes—is conscious, deliberate mental
activity. Students can't daydream, doze off, or fidget while
writing" (1979, 17).

WRITING TO MAKE LEARNING PERSONAL

The kinds of writing my students did over *Time Piece* British
researcher James Britton (1975) has called "expressive writing."
It is personal, private, and intensely inward. The words and
meanings expressed typically communicate more to the creator
of them than to a reader. Rather than the language used at
the podium, expressive writing is the language of our daily,
unpressured speech, what we use when talking to those we
know well, including ourselves. It is what we use when trying
to explain something for the first time. Initial drafts are largely
composed of expressive writing. We're concerned with making
meaning for ourselves; we're unconcerned with how others
will perceive us.

Expressive writing is seminal and therefore crucial to growth
not only in writing, but also to learning in general. Britton's

colleagues, Nancy Martin, Pat D'Arcy, Bryan Newton, and Robert Parker, assert that it is through expressive writing that we make personal links between what we already know and what we are trying to learn (1976, 26).

These personal links help us establish a vested interest in our learning. What is impersonal we must somehow make personal. Then we learn well. Expressive writing, an individual voice deliberately working to create meaning, is as personal as you can get. It is a tool available to students; it is a tool available to teachers. And its use has been neglected too long in secondary schools.

One problem of learning any content-area subject matter is dealing with unfamiliar terminology, vocabulary that embodies key concepts. Whether the term is *manifest destiny, photosynthesis, isosceles triangle, account debits, double dribble,* or *cross-stitching,* we want students to start using it, thinking with it, wondering with it. Merely listening to the teacher say the word, writing it once or twice in class notes, and encountering it on a test is not enough to solidify understanding. Expressive writing offers an excellent way to let students practice using new terms and start to make them part of their personal knowledge.

One junior in his response to *Time Piece* wrote:

> This movie was very confussing. One moment your in a hospital the next your walking through the woods dressed like Tarzan. Maybe this movie is trying to tell us how time controls our lives. It was a very difficult to figure out what in the hell was going on. Maybe the movie was there to give us a good laugh. Or maybe the filmaker was using a type of juxtapose to give us a third meaning, I just don't know what.

Amid the errors of grammar, spelling, and punctuation in this response, some significant learning is beginning. The student tries a first, beautifully stumbling attempt at making the language of film editing his language: "maybe the filmaker was using a type of juxtapose to give us a third meaning. . . ." His use of *third meaning* is correct. He errs when he uses *juxtapose* instead of *juxtaposition.* But oh, what an exciting, risk-taking, learning-leap error it is—one to make a teacher's heart flutter (like mine did), one to be commended, not single-mindedly corrected.

Expressive writing is not for marking or grading or evaluating against some unattainable, ideal performance. It is writing produced by students who have been cut loose, who have been freed from the restraints of artificial forms. Students who are fearless in producing expressive writing realize that they may err without suffering the chopping block. Their teachers encourage them to follow their language-driven, high-powered thinking wherever it may lead. And although this kind of writing is of most worth to the ones who produce it, students who write it believe that honest, forthright thinking on their part will also be valued by their teachers and peers.

WRITING TO GET READY TO LEARN

I often use expressive writing when introducing topics for reading and study. I want to involve students personally, to alert their "perceptual expectations" (Barnes 1976, 87) to the upcoming material, to let them discover what they already know. It doesn't matter what concept is about to be studied. It could be the digestive system, or neon, or abolitionists, or three-dimensional perspective. In the following example, the topic was one Thoreau wrote about in *Walden*. Before my students read his chapter titled "Reading," I had them write for ten minutes about their attitude toward the subject. One bright high-school junior surprised me with this:

> Reading takes me away. When I read Ragtime I was in such awe of the time and people & everything I sped through tuning out everything around me. I always check out the newspaper to see what's going on, and most evenings you'll see me listening to the TV with my nose stuck in a magazine. Magazines offer short passages (I hate long ones) and often talk about things I'm curious about. But I never read the fictional stories. I just never seem interested in them. In my opinion I like writing that has opinions. that is writing by a person so I might see how the person is behind the words. And not the typist. Reading is a chore if I'm not intrested, but when I'm into it you can't hardly get me out of it.

Maybe that's why if someone asks me if I like reading, I say no.

Laurie Waczula, junior

It is not my duty to persuade Laurie that she must surely like reading since she reads so well, or that she, one of my best students, cannot possibly mean that last sentence. And it would be grossly inappropriate for me to correct her usage and punctuation in this kind of quick freewriting. I hadn't asked her to produce flawless, error-free prose. No, I had asked her to pursue at full speed her thoughts about reading, concentrating on nothing but her thinking and where that thinking might lead her. In this instance, it led to a vivid, full-voiced account of her reading habits and preferences, capped by a surprising concluding statement of stunning finality.

The act of writing had done all I'd hoped. It had given her what Robert Frost said the writing of each of his poems had given him: "the occasion for a fresh think" (Clarke, 1967). With language, Laurie had focused intensely upon her subject. The results were not blurry thoughts or vague feelings. Quite the opposite. She had written bold statements about her subject and was now ready to read what someone else had written about it. The freewriting was of value to her, *whether I read it or not.* But I did happen to read this assignment and thus discovered what characteristic of a writer most commanded Laurie's respect. Later, I was not surprised to learn that she liked Thoreau.

Such an assignment represents writing done to get ready to read or study—a pump priming of the first order. Any teacher in any classroom could use such focused writing before beginning a lecture, introducing a new topic, assigning a reading selection. I use such connecting-writing frequently. Sometimes we share the pieces in large or small groups. Sometimes I collect the papers, read them, and select a few to read aloud the following day. Sometimes I do neither. Again, this writing is of most benefit to the students, not me. They know that I respect what they say, and they know that what they say will stand, not as the final say, but as their say. And after they've written, I know they're keyed to what we're about to study.

WRITING TO EXERCISE INTELLECTUAL INDEPENDENCE

Of even more value, I think, is the use of expressive writing *after* or *while* students are learning. Such writing gives students time to sort their impressions and think independently. During class discussions, I prefer to avoid the domino effect—the phenomenon that occurs when one student states an opinion emphatically and all the opinions after that one fall right in behind, unremarkably similar. Fulwiler (1985) points out that expressive writing "allows the writer to explore the issue without being directed first by other people's opinions" (58). In a classroom full of peer pressure–conscious teenagers, such private exploration before public discussion is almost mandatory.

When we studied documentary filmmaking, I showed my students *If You Love This Planet* (Nash 1982), the controversial Canadian film in which Dr. Helen Caldicott documents the medical effects of nuclear war and takes an uncompromising stand against nuclear weapons. I had prepared an evaluation sheet for the students to complete after viewing. But the film was so provocative, so stirring that the only appropriate response to it was something personal, private, and human. We wrote. The students maintained the integrity of their sweet independence, and their words revealed the political and emotional extremes contained in America.

A junior girl:

> I am truly shocked and terrified! I can't believe all of the facts & figures that people don't tell us about. Last year in American studies we saw films of the after effects of the bomb in Hiroshima but when you see them I thought as I'm sure lots of other people did, Oh that can never happen to us.
> But it can and it almost did in 1979 which I didn't know that the world was on a nuclear alert for six minutes. We could have all died and never known what hit us.
> I am physically shaking because the theme of this movie has scared me so much. I have never been told about fall out shelters and what to do in case of a nuclear attack if one was to happen right now all I could

do is sit and wait to die. As a matter of fact I would rather sit and die because there would be no kind of life afterwards for me. I feel that this is a very informative film and I also feel that it shouldn't be shown to young children because I my self am terrified to think this could happen.

Rosalee Marler

A junior boy:

Propaganda!! This lady was so one sided it wasn't funny, plus she gave incorrect information about things in history. For one, we didn't drop the bomb on hiroshima to test it on humans we did it because the Japenese gov't did not want to surrender. We informed them about this bomb but they still woundn't surrender, so we dropped it. With Nagsaki she said she didn't understand why we dropped two nuclear bombs. It is because the Japenese gov't didn't want to surrender even after Hiroshima that is why we dropped two. Once again she *lies*, about history when she stated Russia not breaking any agreement or treaties. This is false. Russia has broken nearly everyone of the treaties they have signed with us.

Marty Daughetee

For this particular film, I took time to let all the students share their thinking by reading what they had written. No dominoes fell. The classroom atmosphere was charged with opinions, questions, and a dozen different slants to a similar position. Never had I experienced such riveted attention on the part of students. I received each writer's words and sometimes asked a clarifying question. When discussion followed the sharing of a piece of writing, I mediated, kept the talk from falling into chaos, pressed for understanding and mutual respect.

After the period ended, I found myself drained by this exhilarating class hour in which students thought, voiced those thoughts, and listened to others voice theirs. It exemplified education in a democratic society. And such a class wouldn't have occurred, I'm convinced, had I merely opened the floor for discussion after showing the film. Many students would have remained mute. I've seen it happen. The ten minutes of writing time, however, allowed for personal reflection and the working out of feelings and ideas swirling in their minds. This, in turn, bolstered (and, in some cases, created) the confidence for students to speak their thinking, their writing, their words.

WRITING TO WONDER

In addition to using the power of written language to make personal sense of learning experiences, students can also use writing to make predictions about future learning. Reading teachers have long known that making predictions about what may lie ahead in the text leads to better reading comprehension. Predicting can also lead to better concept comprehension in any subject area.

Such predicting or conjecturing isn't alien to us. In fact, people have a penchant for it. Martin et al. point out that "we do [it] continuously in conversation about people, events and ideas" (86). Everybody spends time guessing, wondering, constructing scenarios, and speculating. Classroom teachers can put this natural inclination to work by letting students use writing to conjecture about outcomes, strategies, and hypothetical situations. When given opportunities to use the generative power of writing to conjecture about information and concepts, students become actively involved in learning, in creating understandings for themselves.

After my daughter, then thirteen, had read fifty pages of *To Kill a Mockingbird* one summer, I asked her to write expressively for twenty minutes, saying anything she pleased about the characters and plot, conjecturing whenever she could.

> Boo Radley (Mr. Aurther) I'm not sure is really alive. If he is I think he put the gum & The Indian head pennies for Sout & Jem to find. I think he watches them play, and he may want to come out but he's not allowed to or he thinks they'll think he's strange or something. Atticus is a very smart man, he knows what's right &

wrong, he had a right to tell Jem, Dill & Sout not to play games to make fun of Boo & also to stop bothering the Radleys house. Old Mr. Radley's sort of strange, he walks by & coughs on his way to town is quiet & doesn't communicate with anyone. Dill is a very full-of-shit person: he tells tails like anything, maybe it helps him think better of himself Sout & Jem seem to like him.

Calpurina is a pretty wise hip woman who is the cook etc. of the house. She knows the kids well enough to know what they're doing. I'm really not sure what's going to happen. I think the Key to the story is how Jem brakes his arm. Maybe they get Boo Radley out or they enter the house uninvited. Someone is in the house watching because when Scout wall rolling in the tire & crashed she thought she heard someone laughing in the house. The outcome of the story is questionable.

Mariana Romano

Plenty of junior-high students could produce such writing. It is routine in many ways, containing a full complement of spelling errors, run-on sentences, and comma splices. But if readers look only at the breaches of writing etiquette, they will miss the significant thinking that took place during the twenty minutes of written discussion and conjecturing.

Mariana begins by leisurely recounting some of the plot elements and obvious details of characterization. Nothing striking. But this kind of uneventful shoveling and sifting is necessary to set up circumstances whereby she might strike something of value, which she does in discussing Scout and Jem's precocious friend: "Dill is a very full-of-shit person: he tells tails like anything, maybe it helps him think better of himself."

Although some readers may not approve of my daughter's diction, I urge her to stake a claim on the vein of inferential thinking she's struck. Her interpretation of Dill's propensity for fabrication is as sound as any scholar's.

A few lines later, when it seems that Mariana is nearly out of conjectures, her linguistic digging reveals another rich find: "I think the Key to the story is how Jem brakes his arm." She's creating meaning for herself in this exploratory writing, putting pieces of information together, making sense. It's at once routine and extraordinary. All human beings can do it, and the doing of it is positively exhilarating.

In his semiautobiographical novel, *Martin Eden*, Jack London comments upon what it's like to write with exploration as a goal. Of young Martin's voracious pursuit of knowledge through reading and writing, London writes, "Never had the spirit of adventure lured him more strongly than on this amazing exploration of the realm of mind" ([1909] 1922, 95).

The quest of the mind's contents is a spirited business all right, stimulating to engage in, thrilling to behold. Big issues come to the fore; trifles fall away. So hot is my daughter's pursuit of her thoughts and recollections, for example, that in the next-to-last sentence, her mind racing ahead of her hand, intent to get down what she is discovering, she finishes one word with the middle letters of the next: ". . . when Scout *wall rolling* in the tire. . . ." To correct such a glorious error in this circumstance would be ludicrous. The stains on my daughter's clothing are inconsequential while she's at work mining the mountain.

WRITING TO STRUGGLE WITH DIFFICULT LEARNING

Honest labor. Too often it is neglected in our classrooms. Too often students aren't required to work for knowledge. Teachers pose questions. Students stare blankly. The usuals stab at answers. The majority say nothing. Are they thinking about possible answers? You can't be sure. But it doesn't matter; you end up giving the answer anyway.

And yet we know from experience that attaining something through effort is more valuable, more meaningful than having it handed over. We didn't learn to become effective teachers by sitting in teacher-education classes. We had to enter class-rooms, plan strategies, do tough-minded thinking about goals and methods; and, above all, we had to work with students. Intellectual struggle with real chances to succeed is healthy. And that's why students must have plenty of opportunities to dig in and slug it out with knotty problems. Such struggle will sharpen their thinking ability and net them real knowledge.

Through writing, through concentrated examination with language, students can engage in productive mental struggles that will empower them and create solid learning. To illustrate, I recount the story of Rhonda, a sophomore, the first of her class to finish *To Kill a Mockingbird*. Immediately, she came to my desk, where I sat reading.

"Mr. Romano, what happened at the end?"

"Which part specifically?"

"Who killed who?"

"Wasn't it clear?"

"I couldn't figure it out."

I gazed out over the classroom full of sophomores, about half of them looking up expectantly from their books. "I'll tell you what, Rhonda—you go write about it, then we'll talk."

Rhonda was used to such grappling writing. She went to work and fifteen minutes later brought this paper to me:

> The ending was sort of confusing but then I figured out that Boo Radley saved Jem & Scout from Bob Ewell.
>
> I liked when Mrs. Maudie put the snooty Mrs. Merriweather in her place.
>
> Scout was an excellent character.—She had alot of different moods.
>
> I read the end over again slowly and now I understand that Boo killed Bob Ewell with a kitchen knife. The sheriff took the switchblade from Bob Ewell when he found him dead and realized what happened. The sheriff belived Boo was innocent because he saved Jem & Scout from Boo Ewell.
>
> *Rhonda Lawson*

Rhonda had not done what I'd asked. She had not written without stopping. She explained to me that after she wrote the third paragraph, she thought of the switchblade. "It didn't make any sense to me when I read it the first time," said Rhonda, "so I went back and reread those pages and figured it out." She smiled triumphantly. And I cherished this opportunity to witness full literacy in motion, the complementary to-and-fro of reading and writing.

I showed this sophomore's paper to my daughter, told her how Rhonda hadn't been able to figure out the ending until

deep thinking of the plot events through writing.
liked *To Kill a Mockingbird*. She read with interest
ents of another, older teenager.

pa," she said, "the girl wrote *Boo* Ewell at the
of *Bob* Ewell."

ᴵ was shocked at my daughter's pedantry. "I'm surprised
at you, Mariana. You know she meant *Bob*. She was just all
caught up in her meaning."

"I know that," said Mariana. "What I mean is that in the
beginning of the book everybody thinks Boo is the bad guy.
I even thought he might murder somebody. But in the end
it's Bob who's the real villain. So it kind of makes sense—
Boo Ewell."

My indignation turned to chagrin. "I see what you mean."

Perception. Conjecture. Error. Knowledge. They are com-
patriots. In *Blue Highways* William Least Heat Moon writes,
"If a man can keep alert and imaginative, an error is a possibility,
a chance at something new; to him, wandering and wondering
are part of the same process, and he is most mistaken, most
in error, whenever he quits exploring" (1982, 223–24). I don't
know what Rhonda's subconscious was doing as she began to
write purposefully about *To Kill a Mockingbird*, nailing down
her understanding of its denouement, but my daughter's interpretation of the unintentional error is intriguing. Mariana,
Rhonda, writing, thinking, meaning, and error met at a place
where only active participation and interaction could take
them. The place is called Learning.

WRITING TO ENGAGE THE IMAGINATION IN LEARNING

Conjecturing as my daughter did in her writing and thinking
needs to be part of every student's learning style in every
subject area from vocational agriculture to physics. Teachers
should create opportunities for students to actively practice
speculation. Furthermore, if teachers are really interested in
fostering learning, they will make room in their classes for
conjecturing's powerful parent—imagination. Martin et al.
maintain that unless students are encouraged "to use their
imaginations more extensively, their knowledge will remain
inert" (86). And they are not referring merely to the knowledge

learned in English class. Imagination should be a welcome guest in classrooms throughout the secondary school.

In every discipline information heaps up, begins to overwhelm. Facts become dry and tedious:

Alveoli are the tiny air sacs of the lungs.

Alveoli take oxygen inhaled and pass it into the bloodstream.

Alveoli remove carbon dioxide from the bloodstream and pass it back to the lungs for expulsion.

Martin et al. explain that only when students are able to somehow "put themselves in the picture" are they "likely to perceive the significance of the facts at their disposal" (86). To put students in the picture, teachers may ask them to adopt a persona and write a first-person narrative from that point of view. A student might become a drop of gasoline as it travels through an engine, a volleyball sick and tired of being used by nincompoops who won't abide by the rules of the game, a fine piece of oak in the hands of a master woodworker, a water molecule in a piece of chicken placed in a microwave oven. Such writing assignments provide students with a refreshing, imaginative jolt. They must leave their narrow, too-comfortable perspective and consider concepts from a new one. They must close their eyes to their familiar way of seeing and open them to a new way.

A colleague of mine, health-education teacher Tom Thomas, gave his students such an imaginative jolt after they had studied the respiratory system and the effects of cigarette smoking. A tenth grader responded with this:

> "My lungs aren't as good as they were when I was a baby." There's the big shot shooting off his mouth again. I wish he did my job for one day, then he'd stop breathing that smoke and start breathing some air.
>
> I don't think I'm asking too much, all I want is some oxygen for my friends, the red blood cells. They come in here all the time for oxygen and I give them all I have, but it isn't enough, because of all the black, sticky tar covering me. I can't absorb as much oxygen as I used to, so everyday I work twice as hard as the day before to give the red blood cells the oxygen they need to stay alive. Another thing this hot shot takes a bath 3 times a day so he can look "clean for the ladies." I haven't been clean since he started smoking and that

was 5 years ago. Let's see him go without a bath for a
week, then he'll get a small taste of my life in the tar
pit.

Everyone down here has given that dipstick hints.
First we made his teeth yellow, he gets TOPAL. Then
we let loose of the stink bombs on his breath, he gets
CLORETS. Next we made him have a coughing spell on
the tennis court in front of the ladies; they covered him
with affection. We've finally took a vote in the Aveoli
Union.

We the Aveoli Union have resolved that, if we don't
see some action out of this turkey we're going to strike,
maybe that will get him to stop smoking those tar sticks.

Linette Sands

All the examples of student writing I've quoted in this
chapter, except the one above, have been produced in English
classes. I wish I had more content areas represented. I wish
I had samples of expressive writing from biology, physics,
and art; from home economics, history, and math. But they
are hard to come by.

"It's not our job to teach writing," a content-area teacher
once said to me. And he was right. In fact, I don't particularly
want content-area teachers doing much *teaching* of writing.
That's mainly our baby, we English teachers who study writing,
read writing, and write writing.

But I would like to see content-area teachers *using* writing.
And I'd like to see them using it for more than merely testing
students with essay prompts, book reports, and short-answer
questions. Although writing is certainly useful for revealing
information learned, it is even more useful for learning information. Students who readily and habitually use their personal language for learning possess a most powerful educational
tool. And teachers can put this tool in students' hands. They
can have them write to discover, create, and explore their
thinking, to dig up prior knowledge, to cultivate intellectual
independence, to conjecture about possibilities, to struggle
with difficult concepts, and to engage the imagination as an
ally in learning.

Writing for such reasons makes us use language, and using
language makes us think.

REFERENCES

Applebee, Arthur N. 1982. *Writing in the Secondary School: English and the Content Areas*. NCTE Research Report No. 21. Urbana, IL: National Council of Teachers of English.

Barnes, Douglas. 1976. *From Communication to Curriculum*. New York: Penguin Books.

Britton, James. 1975. "The Composing Processes and the Functions of Writing." In *Children and Writing in the Elementary School: Theories and Techniques*, edited by Richard L. Larson. New York: Oxford University Press.

Clarke, Shirley (producer). 1967. *A Lover's Quarrel with the World* (Robert Frost documentary film). Pyramid, distributor.

Elbow, Peter. 1983. "Teaching Thinking by Teaching Writing." *Change* 15 (September):37–40.

Fulwiler, Toby. 1979. "Journal Writing Across the Curriculum." In *How to Handle the Paper Load*, edited by Gene Stanford. Urbana, IL: National Council of Teachers of English.

———. 1983. "Why We Teach Writing in the First Place." In *Fforum: Essays on Theory and Practice in the Teaching of Writing*, edited by Patricia L. Stock. Upper Montclair, NJ: Boynton/Cook.

———. 1985. "Writing and Learning, Grade Three." *Language Arts* 62 (January):55–59.

Henson, Jim (director). 1965. Produced by Muppets, Inc. *Time Piece*. Contemporary Films, distributor.

Kuhns, William, and Stanley, Robert. 1969. *Exploring the Film*. Fairfield, NJ: Cebco Standard Publishing.

Lee, Harper. 1960. *To Kill a Mockingbird*. New York: Popular Library.

London, Jack. 1922. *Martin Eden*. New York: The Macmillan Co. (Originally published in 1909.)

Martin, Nancy; D'Arcy, Pat; Newton, Bryan; and Parker, Robert. 1976. *Writing & Learning Across the Curriculum, 11–16*. Upper Montclair, NJ: Boynton/Cook.

Moon, William Least Heat. 1982. *Blue Highways: A Journey into America*. New York: Fawcett Crest.

Murray, Donald. 1984. *Write to Learn*. New York: Holt, Rinehart and Winston.

Nash, Terri (director). 1982. *If You Love This Planet*. National Film Board of Canada, distributor.

Newkirk, Thomas. 1986. "Introduction." In *To Compose: Teaching Writing in the High School*, edited by Thomas Newkirk. Portsmouth, NH: Heinemann. (Originally published in 1985 by the Northeast Regional Exchange, Inc., Chelmsford, MA.)

Thoreau, Henry David. 1962. *Walden and Other Writings*. New York: Bantam Books. (*Walden* originally published in 1854.)

Please Write

A few years ago *English Journal* published an editorial that strongly urged English teachers to write. They really weren't being professional, the author contended, if they taught writing but didn't themselves write, didn't compose at least two pieces a year that they sent out for publication. An English teacher I knew then was indignant about the editorial. He had taught for more than twenty years and had gotten along fine without writing.

"You don't have to publish novels to be a good critic of them," he said. "And you don't have to write in order to teach students to write. I recognize good writing when I see it. And I know when my students produce it and when they do not."

The matter appeared closed, like a teacher's briefcase in summer. But I thought I'd try to jimmy it back open. "Maybe," I said, "the author thinks you'll gain insights about what students go through to produce a piece of writing, if you go through it yourself."

"I *know* what students go through," he said. "I was *once* a student."

He had stated the problem precisely. He no longer saw himself as a student, as a curious learner. Comfortable and static in his "wisdoom," he studied neither his students nor his profession.

"Well," I offered, with more knowledge of what I was about to say than I wanted to admit, "getting an article rejected does make you humble."

's one thing I don't need," he replied, "it's humility.
enough."

tte I couple with a more recent one. Near the
ᴄᴜ-service presentation I conducted in Hamilton
ᴄᴛy, Ohio, I had the teachers write. I wrote with them.
When the writing was done, we talked. One young woman,
perhaps twenty-two or twenty-three, raised her hand. "The
atmosphere in the room really made me want to write," she
said. "How can I create that in my classroom?"

Some of the audience members and I made suggestions:
respecting and valuing students' voices; making sure their
writing is shared with real audiences; installing writing as a
natural, regular part of the class; and, of course, writing along
with the students.

"Do you write with your students?" one teacher asked the
young woman.

"No," she said and averted her eyes. Her voice made the
one word sound like an abject confession. My heart sank for
her.

After my presentation, the young woman came up to me,
where I stood gathering my materials. She spoke with sincerity
and intelligence. Her dark eyes brimmed with enthusiasm.

"I've just been teaching four weeks," she said.

"Then you're right in the thick of it."

She nodded. "You know, I wanted to write with my students,
but my department head advised me not to."

"Why?"

"She said I shouldn't write with the students since I was
just starting out and was so close to their age."

We talked some about a teacher's need to demonstrate the
behavior she desires in her students; about building trust;
about the benefit of knowing firsthand what students feel when
they write, share, and revise. I did not tell the young woman
to defy her department head's advice. "This is an important
year for you," I said. "Do what's comfortable, and keep
studying the kids and learning about your profession."

She nodded and smiled, her eyes still glistening. I felt better
about that moment earlier when she had lowered her head in
embarrassment.

Writing well means writing honestly. The twenty-year English
teacher who could easily determine when his students wrote
well and when they did not knew this. So did the English

department head who blunted some of that young teacher's eagerness by advising her not to write with the students. To be honest on paper is difficult and risky, quite an accomplishment in itself. To then share those true words with others is a profound act of faith and trust. Such writing and sharing require a willingness to become vulnerable.

In a classroom full of opinionated teenagers, the last thing a teacher wants to feel is more vulnerable. The job is tough enough. The twenty-year teacher who needed no humility deemed himself an authority on writing. He had the answers; he had the final word about what was good and what was not. He intended to keep it that way.

The young teacher's department head knew that inexperienced teachers are already prime examples of vulnerability. She thought, I'm sure, that she was doing the new teacher a favor by curbing her impulse to write with students. Maybe she had a point. I can't help feeling, however, that the young teacher, so eager and intelligent, could have written with her students and still have found her way to a successful year, might even have *written* her way to a successful year. I thought she was already advanced in the teaching profession—so young, so knowledgeable and open, so willing to take risks.

I had taught for nearly two years before I was bold enough to share my writing with students. Part of my fear was due to a gun-shyness I'd picked up in college freshman English and advanced composition, where student papers were often used for target practice. But a larger part of my timidity arose from my phony pose as a teacher-expert and my fraudulent approach to teaching writing.

In those early years I was the corrector, letting no error I caught slip by. Even the best papers left my desk with a multitude of red pen markings. I genuinely wanted the quality of students' papers to improve in content and meaning, but my numerous red marks showed students that I was most concerned about strict adherence to standard usage, correct orthography, and rules of punctuation. These amenities of writing were not just an important part of the writing process; they were all-important.

Thus, when I first started to demonstrate concepts of written composition with my own work, I brought in only highly polished pieces, writing I felt was beyond the reproach of those high-school writers. As early as 1973 I was a teacher of

was writing and sharing that writing, but I was
ely to prove to students that I was qualified to
vriting. . . .
clever your teacher is, kids?
vell he writes!
now spotless his prose is. No bothersome errors
here as there are in *your* papers.

Later in my teaching, as my focus in evaluation gave more
emphasis to meaning and less to conventions, especially in
the early stages of writing, I not only brought in my finished
written products, but also their various drafts, which I photocopied or put on transparencies so we could discuss them.
Sharing a series of drafts with students is a valuable activity,
since many of them have little notion about how a piece of
writing evolves. And I'd like to believe that I brought those
drafts in primarily to demonstrate such evolution, but I know
different. My examples of evolving writing were mainly to
show students how I eventually came out on top. . . .

See, kids, he struggles, but he emerges a winner!

Note the shine and the fine lines of the final product.

Still later, I developed the courage to bring in first drafts—
unfinished messes containing real dilemmas: problems of word
choice, clarity, focus, and structure. And since I'd done little
polishing or editing, errors of written convention were rife,
especially spelling, one of my fundamental weaknesses. The
revealing of my own writing dilemmas made me more sensitive
to those of my students. But I make no bones about it. By
the time I could share these samples of raw writing I was
seven or eight years out of college, and my confidence had
grown. That young teacher from Hamilton County, Ohio,
was way ahead of me.

The sharing of my messes, my writing under construction,
had a salutary effect on classroom atmosphere. I came to look
upon my students differently. From a judge ready to pronounce
sentence I metamorphosed into an advocate of student writers,
a helper and fellow crafter. And their view of me changed.
They began to perceive me as one who wrote and knew about
writing, not merely as someone who was a stickler for standard
usage and punctuation and who always had in mind an ideal
way of writing something. The teacher, they saw, wrestled
with the same problems they did—a comforting fact for a
learner.

It was even longer before I took the next step in demystifying writing: to sit with pen and paper, compose while the students did, and then read them what I'd written. And it was longer still before I could take the final step. Most students have seen teachers in art, woodworking, or music demonstrate their composing techniques. They've seen teachers mold wet clay at a potter's wheel, shape wood at a lathe, and make music with a saxophone. But few students have seen English teachers write anything more than hall passes or homework assignments. When I was finally able to use an overhead projector to demonstrate the actual generation of written language that sought to make meaning and carry along a reader, I removed the last vestige of mystery from writing.

Truth replaced hocus-pocus. It is human beings who create those first words, false starts, scratched-out lines, and messy pages that eventually become polished writing published in books and magazines. And those human beings are not so unlike the freshmen in your final class of the day.

The fundamental humanness of writing was taught to me during my undergraduate study in the classes of Milton White, a writer of fiction whose teaching and writing styles were identical—both lean, elegant, witty, and compassionate. Unable to get enough of his benign influence, I enrolled in four of his upper-level writing courses. During each class meeting we discussed the stories of three or four students, with Milton weaving in his experience-won perceptions of writing. More than once he said that writing was like removing one's clothing. I found the idea both provocative and embarrassing. One day, as each student's story was discussed, I successfully imagined him or her sitting naked at the seminar table. Provocative indeed! But a few days later I found the idea most embarrassing when it was time for the class to discuss my story.

Good writing, Milton taught us, reveals the writer, exposes him. Readers get close, lingering looks. The better the reader, the closer the look. And it isn't merely the external blemishes and beauty marks they see. Readers peer into the writer's very soul. They judge the depth of sensitivity, the clearness of thinking, the soundness of values, and the range and sophistication of verbal skill. If beauty and truth embody the writer's spirit, they will be revealed. So, too, will shallowness and ineptitude.

In a letter to Peter Benchley, John Steinbeck wrote, "The

written word punishes both stupidity and dishonesty" (1975, 490). Learning to write well is exacting. It is hard work for both students and professional writers. Unlike professional writers, however, students possess neither the vast experience to see them through writing slumps nor the luxury of an editor to alert them to the bits of stupidity and dishonesty that inevitably creep into writing.

And never is it more agonizing to appear stupid or dishonest than during the teen years. But in attempting to write well-said truths, in trying to say what we mean, we invariably stumble, hedge, and write awkwardly. Teenage writers must realize that it's all right to do this, that it's necessary to reveal flaws on the way to presenting the best self. Before we don our nattiest attire, we must stand unclad before the mirror. But we dress. We dress.

Although an inevitable part of writing, errors and failures are not insurmountable. They need not be all-defeating. Sensitive, knowledgeable teachers can serve as excellent examples to show students this. Of course, to do so, teachers must write and share that writing, flaws and all. They must show students their writing samples that reveal wordiness, unfocused thoughts, unnecessarily complicated sentences, and routine errors of writing etiquette. Amid this writing that has so far gone wrong will also be lucid phrases, striking lines, and clear thinking. These, too, are shared.

I once asked a group of third graders in Jan Roberts's Lee, New Hampshire, classroom to write about writing. They were free to say anything they chose about any aspect of their writing. Many of the children volunteered to read what they'd written. A discussion ensued that soon exploded into argument. One faction, spearheaded by the boys, maintained that the writer's emotions weren't even remotely related to what he wrote. "Writing," pronounced their spokesman, "has nothing to do with feelings."

One of the girls bristled at this. She rose from her chair, fixed penetrating blue eyes on her classmate, and said, "Writing *is* feelings. When you write, you write your feelings."

I'm inclined to agree with her. Writing is feelings, surely feelings bound up with intellect and personality, but feelings nonetheless. If teachers expect students to reveal these feelings, to psychically disrobe, then lines of trust must crisscross the classroom. The students must trust themselves. They must trust each other. And they must trust the teacher.

An impossible task, given the social cliques of teenagers? Completely, yes. But students can learn to trust themselves, the teacher, and enough of their classmates so that a productive writing community is created, one with enough support to make teenagers want to write, one in which they are comfortable enough to take risks. The teacher is the first and most convincing example of the kind of behavior she wants in her class. She writes honestly, she shares what she's written, she listens to the writing of her students and respects their voices and visions.

A fourth grader once told me what it meant to her when she saw her teacher, Phyllis Kinzie, writing in class. "Writing's not just for children," said the girl. "It's for everybody." Not just professional writers who make a living at it, not just high-school students assigned compositions. When teachers bend over a piece of paper with pen in hand, when they read aloud rough words they've written for some real purpose, when they compose on the overhead or chalkboard, they send their students an important message. It reads, "Writing is for all people. I am with you." The message soon becomes a tacit classroom maxim. Students know the teacher's passion for writing. They know she respects writers. And they know that in her class they are writers.

Writing is learned only through participation. Teachers who write and share their words assume a humane, participatory stance toward learning and teaching the craft of writing. Such a stance does not deal in absolutes or ideal choices. Teacher-writers are not so much experts as they are practitioners who are continuing to learn how to write. They are willing to read their final drafts to students. And, more importantly, they are willing to produce raw writing and share it with students, sans the second and third vision, sans the tightening and polishing of language.

A participatory stance. Young writers learn best from teachers who write, just as children learning to swim learn best from teachers who actually get into the water with them. Empathy makes a sensitive teacher. Knowledge born of doing is firm. Teachers who merely pace the pool deck, shouting dicta and theories are not nearly as effective as those who participate regularly, who continually renew their knowledge and empathy.

Writing teachers must participate often and for as many reasons as possible. They must swim sprints until they are left standing at the shallow end of the pool, gasping for air. They must swim a choppy sea when a rhythm won't come and a sudden, swallowed mouthful of water leaves them sputtering and coughing. They must risk looking ungainly as they try a new flip-turn technique. And, occasionally, they must swim long distances, emerging from the pool weary yet satisfied. Then, when students are in the water, teachers will understand their struggles, their failures, their progress and triumphs because they have lived them too.

Not long ago, in a classroom of juniors and seniors, I brought in the first draft of a poem I had begun (Figure 3–1) and placed it on the overhead projector. In addition to demonstrating once again to students that their teacher did indeed write on his own time, I also wanted to show them what initial, groping writing looked like. In my own hand I had transcribed the unfinished, incipient poem onto a transparency, remaining faithful to all my initial scratch-outs, line breaks, wordiness, and diction. On the screen was my wonderful mess in my own hand.

One student immediately asked who the *you* was in the first line. The *you*, I told her, was each of my students.

"Is that edge you're talking about the cliff's edge, like you wrote at the bottom?"

"Yes."

"So that means you want to kill us?"

"No, I don't want to kill you. I don't mean it that way. I just want you to enter a danger zone, be completely left on your own so you have to find your own ways to learn."

"But if it's a cliff you push us over, you'll kill us."

"Well, I don't want to harm you, but I do want you to take some risks. Falling off a cliff is the image that popped into my mind when I was reading your pieces."

"It's drastic," said another student.

All the students were silent a moment, gazing up at the screen.

"Anything strike you in the poem, George?"

"Yeah, I like *lurking*—sounds sneaky."

"Yeah, *cling*'s good too, but how about *push*? Makes me think of pushy people."

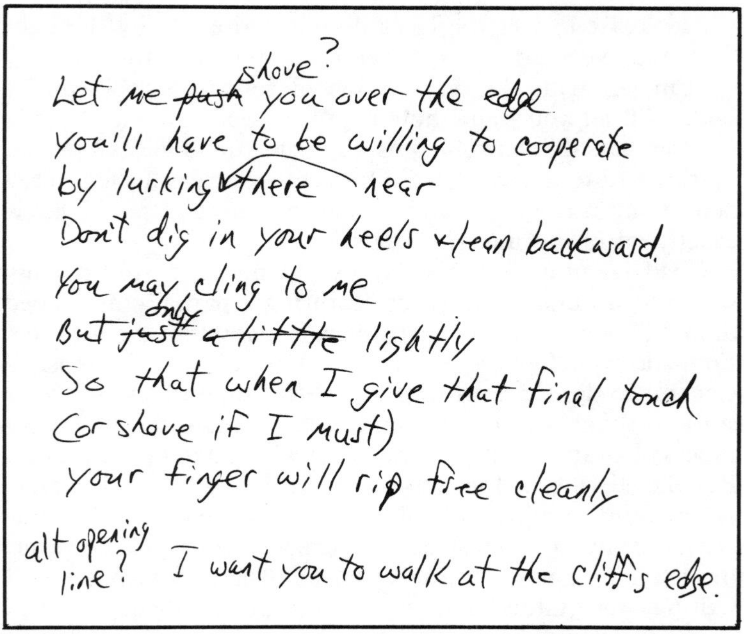

Let me ~~push~~ shove? you over the edge
you'll have to be willing to cooperate
by lurking ~~there~~ near
Don't dig in your heels ×lean backward.
You may cling to me
But ~~just~~ only ~~a little~~ lightly
So that when I give that final touch
(or shove if I must)
your finger will rip free cleanly
alt opening line? I want you to walk at the cliff's edge.

FIGURE 3-1

"*Shove* is worse, though," said another. "I'd rather be pushed than shoved."

"I don't wanna be either."

"I've got *touch* up there too," I said. "I'd rather learning be that way, but sometimes I have to push kids into it. Sometimes I have to push myself into it. Learning can be scary, but I want everything to end all right for my students."

"That's gonna be hard if you push them over a cliff."

"That's the problem I've got to work out. See, the more we've written in here, the more I've been thinking about you guys taking risks in the way you write and what you write about. To grow, you have to try new things, think new things. That can be risky, even dangerous—the cliff image probably came out of that. I can't jump over the cliff for you, so I'm thinking maybe my job as a teacher is to give each of you a push, if you need it. Anyone see what I mean?"

I looked out over the faces illuminated eerily by the light from the overhead. No one ventured a comment.

"I'm left with the writer's job of solving a problem," I said. "I'll let you know how it progresses."

After class that day one quiet girl came up to me as I wound up the cord to the overhead. One sentence was all she uttered before she turned and went on to her next class. "I knew exactly what you meant," she said.

I had taken a risk that day by sharing with students my writing—an unfinished poem featuring a partially developed thought about a subject that was personally important to me. I'd made myself vulnerable, as Ken Macrorie (1974) has asked teachers to do. I'd leapt from the cliff. I didn't have a success story to share with the students. At that point in my writing process I wasn't at all sure the poem would end up successful. But the sharing had let me—and the students—look closely at emerging writing. We all saw that I needed to do some clarifying in my almost-poem. Just as important, however, the students got a glimpse of an adult amid the process of writing, not quite saying what he meant, but struggling and groping, talking about it, working on writing that hadn't been assigned to him.

Through me they saw real-world writing demonstrated. Samples of published writing can do this too, but they sometimes carry the weight of intimidation, the hint that this is something only professionals do. We need to put writing in the hands of the people—all of them, a tool for their use. A classroom teacher can demonstrate dramatically how a flesh-and-blood person puts a variety of writing genres to useful work in our society.

Over the years I've shared with my students all kinds of writing I've done for many different purposes. Through a journal entry shared five years after I wrote it, my students learned about the death of my beloved uncle and how it hit me. They heard a short story I based upon an evening spent with my daughter, then twelve, sleeping beneath the stars. They evaluated my letters, one to Marathon Oil, complaining of shoddy work performed at one of their service stations (which gained me an eleven-dollar refund); and another to the Cincinnati *Enquirer*, lamenting the decision to serve spicy brown mustard only in the expensive, box-seat sections of Riverfront Stadium (the attitude of the Cincinnati Reds organization toward fans who sat in the cheaper seats was "Let them eat yellow mustard").

Students have read my memos, announcements, and movie reviews. They have listened to poems I wrote to honor the girls' volleyball team and help spur them to tournament victories. In addition, I have shared fables, essays, limericks, and remembrances. All these writings I composed in my everyday traffic with the world.

Doing them gave me personal satisfaction.

This is yet another reason why I warmly implore teachers to write. As Donald Murray explains, "Teachers should write, first of all, because it is fun. It is a satisfying human activity that extends both the brain and the soul. It stimulates the intellect, deepens the experience of living, and is good therapy" (1985, 73).

We English teachers know well the fun and satisfaction that come with reading. We can all name books that have provoked our thinking and stirred our emotions. We didn't view life in quite the same way after traveling with Jane Eyre or Jay Gatsby, Siddhartha or Randle P. McMurphy. We want our students to be similarly provoked and stirred by literature. We want them to experience the fulfillment and revel in the pleasures of reading. And we cannot conceive of teaching literature without reading widely ourselves.

Writing, of course, is the flip side of literacy. Without writing, there would be nothing to read. If we teachers purport to nurture our students' growth in writing, to have them believe that writing matters in the world, just as reading does, then we ourselves must write. We cannot merely talk about the importance of writing. We must live it. Anything less makes counterfeit the teaching of full literacy, that precious coin of the realm.

A number of years ago, when writing teachers and researchers began to suggest that English teachers in the secondary schools should write, the proposal was met with much resistance. Some was of the sort that I recounted in the beginning of this chapter—teacher as aristocrat, student as peasant. Experienced teachers would never deign to show their writing (if indeed they wrote at all) to unfinished, sometimes crude students; and beginning teachers, if they were to survive, had better start cultivating an aloof, "professional" attitude.

Another sort of resistance arose from the realities of teaching in secondary schools: too many classes, too many students. I did the same calculations that many teachers must have done when they considered and then rejected the idea of writing with students. I work in a high school whose principal does everything in his power to keep class size low, especially in writing courses. Although I have three or four preparations a semester, I teach only five classes with about twenty-five students in each class—good numbers by most high-school standards. Could I possibly write with every class, produce five first drafts, one or two revisions of each, and five final, cleanly typed copies?

Of course not. For a portion of the silent writing time I give my students I need to complete part of my teaching work—recording grades, planning lessons, reading and re-reading literature, evaluating homework, and completing the numerous bits of bureaucratic paperwork that appear in my mailbox. I also need a large chunk of time to circulate through the classroom, conferencing with students about their writing. Anyone who chides teachers for attending to other matters while their students write needs to spend an entire year teaching a full load in a secondary school.

But despite the demands of my job and the impossibility of writing with my students each time they do, I must and can show my students I write. Above all, I can make sure students in every one of my classes actually see me writing a number of times, especially in the beginning of the school year. I may work on my personal writing, or try an assignment I've made, or join students in a focused freewriting over a film we've just seen. It doesn't matter what sort of writing I do.

What does matter is that I am writing in their presence. Should they look up from their papers, they will see my intent look, my moving hand, my sudden stops for reading and brief reflection. I can also use the overhead projector and photocopier to share the writing dilemmas I face and often solve, sometimes with my students' help. And I can demonstrate the high value I place on composing with words by respecting the efforts of anyone who creates with them, whether the writer be Robert Frost or the sophomore in the far corner of the room, squeezing the pencil stub, leaning into the notebook paper.

I do these things and my students know me for a man of the written word, a teacher of reading and writing, a friendly spirit who seeks to push them over the cliffs of literacy. Most of them do not mind the fall. My ultimate goal is that the pushing becomes unnecessary, that they take to leaping from cliffs of their own accord. And thrill in it. So I make the leaps myself. In a secondary-school English class, that means I write and share my writing, just as I ask my students to.

REFERENCES

Macrorie, Ken. 1974. *A Vulnerable Teacher*. Rochelle Park, NJ: Hayden Book Co.

Murray, Donald M. 1985. *A Writer Teaches Writing*. 2d ed., a complete revision. Boston: Houghton Mifflin Co.

Steinbeck, John. 1975. *Steinbeck: A Life in Letters*. Edited by Elaine Steinbeck and Robert Wallsten. New York: Viking Press.

4

Writing Processes in Theory

A writer cooks. Sometimes the heat is turned high. Ripe and sliced, various foods sputter in a hot, concentrated tablespoonful of motivation. The writer adds spice, a personal brand of it, and deftly stirs the ingredients, which exchange flavors and become something together that none could be alone. When the writer sets this dish on the table, readers respond with "oooohs" and "ahhhhs." "This dish," they say with satisfaction, "is pure inspiration."

At other times a writer can barely keep the heat on warm. One meager ingredient tries to simmer. The writer knows that several others are needed to make the dish complete. He's checked different sources and cannot locate what he needs. Furthermore, he's undecided about what spice to use.

But the writer doesn't fret over this dish that won't come together. He attends to other matters—plans future meals, checks something baking in the oven, perhaps even begins another dish on a different burner. Occasionally, however, he comes over to the stove to stir the bland dish, tasting a bit, maybe adding a little salt, a little pepper. Still, he knows there's nothing much of substance there.

The writer keeps coming back to the stove, though, and one time while he's stirring and tasting, he thinks of another ingredient he needs. He adds it quickly. The taste improves just a bit. But more important, the subtle change in flavor and texture now tells him what seasoning to use. The writer's mood lightens as he peels a generous supply of the spice and drops the pieces in, singing in a strong voice all the while.

Now, the dish bubbles slowly. The writer stirs. A distinct and pleasing aroma rises from the pan. This work is satisfying but tiring. He opens the refrigerator, reaches for a cool drink, and by chance discovers an ingredient he had stored away and forgotten. Quickly, he adds it and turns up the heat. He stirs the steaming dish, the bubbles sputtering now. He tastes and frowns. He removes some of the spice he added earlier. He tastes again, this time licks his lips. Perfect. And suddenly he thinks of an ideal complementary side dish.

Just before dinner, the writer wipes the stove to sparkling, sets the table precisely, and opens the wine to breathe. Later that evening, his guests, full and content, lean back in their chairs, sigh, and say, "That dish was pure inspiration."

Meals and pieces of writing come to completion in different ways. Cooks may use similar ingredients and utensils, yet prepare meals that differ vastly. Writers too. They all use pen and paper, often a typewriter, maybe a computer. And although they work in separate kitchens with variously stocked pantries, all writers create with the basic ingredient of language. But each writer has a personal brand of language, and each goes about the writing process uniquely. This is as it should be.

Despite this healthy diversity, writers go through similar processes and often complete them in the same order. All writers come up with ideas. They get these ideas into language on paper. They shape the language, adding, deleting, changing, and rearranging to communicate powerfully their intended and discovered meanings. They rid their writing of errors. They publish their work.

All writers, including student writers, develop a process (or processes) by which they work. Our responsibility as writing teachers is to help students learn personal processes for creating writing that enable them to create their best writing. Products are made by processes. The writing-cooking piece I opened this chapter with, for example, began with my observations of a third grader named Chad as he struggled to write a piece about his dog. I was struck by Chad's struggle because his previous piece about stamp collecting hadn't given him nearly as much trouble.

I decided to write about Chad and the fluency problem he'd encountered. I leafed through my research notes and found the section describing Chad's behavior. As I reread my notes, the cooking metaphor presented itself to me. Like homemade pasta dough, the idea looked promising but needed to be worked with.

I wrote a draft with pen and yellow legal pad (revising occasionally during the drafting).

Next, I gave full attention to revision (drafting new portions as I revised).

Then, I corrected errors (revising here and there as I did).

Finally, I typed the piece (revising just a couple of words and phrases).

The next day I read the finished piece to my research colleagues.

That isn't what you read, though. Five months later, you see, I reread the piece and was amazed to discover so much more I needed to do with it. So I revised for further depth and clarity and sharpened my language. But you didn't read that version either. You read the one I revised and sharpened this morning, ten months later, over a year after Chad's memorable struggle.

Finished writing is produced by a process. With most pieces I write, the process is not nearly as long or involved. In fact, some pieces, like a note to a student or colleague, are completed within minutes, sometimes seconds, with no revision at all. Other pieces take longer, like a poem I've been writing about my father, who died when I was fifteen. I've been working on that for nine years.

It wasn't in English classes that I learned writing processes that worked for me. I had to learn them on my own. Most of my teachers in high school and college emphasized outlining, logic, and correctness. We rarely wrote in class. They tacitly taught a model of the writing process that usually ensured that we would produce ill-conceived, half-realized, and slipshod final products. In those classes I learned the "Due Friday" model of the writing process. It looked something like the scheme shown in Figure 4-1.

Of course, the teachers didn't consciously teach us to write by this process. They didn't teach us to write by *any* process. After they announced a due date, a format, and often a topic, they left us to figure out the mysterious process of producing a final written product. And everyone who turned in the

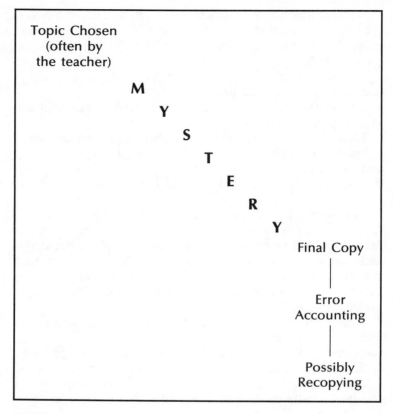

FIGURE 4-1

assignment did indeed develop a process for getting the writing done. For many of us, however, the processes we developed were "dysfunctional" (Calkins 1986, 15).

Many of us never jotted down our ideas before writing. Neither did we talk about our ideas with teacher and peers before or during writing. And always the due date loomed ominously ahead. The closer we got to it, the more overwhelming and intimidating it became. Few of us significantly revised the writing we turned in. Many of us produced a single draft. In college, students often slapped these together at one or two in the morning, sometimes just hours before they were due. In high school, one of my cronies wrote his English papers during first-period American Government. He handed them in second period.

After we turned in our papers, the teachers finally intervened in the writing process. Up to our papers they methodically backed a truck sagging dangerously under its weight of writing dicta, punctuation rules, and usage prescriptions. When the truck was properly positioned, they mechanically raised the bed and dumped the load. Our errors of language, logic, and written convention were accounted for. If we were lucky, we could immediately put the paper out of sight (often in a wastebasket). If we were unlucky, we had to sort through the junk heap and rewrite a new, correct copy.

No doubt, the "Due Friday" model and its variations still exist today. But, happily, the burgeoning of research in the teaching of writing has produced plenty of useful and more accurate models of the writing process. Though such models do not represent *the* way writing is produced, they can help teachers guide students in forming productive strategies for producing their best writing.

One of the most useful models I've found is contained in *Learning to Write/Writing to Learn* (Mayher, Lester, and Pradl 1983). The authors propose that writers go through five stages when producing a piece: *percolating, drafting, revising, editing,* and *publishing*.

Perhaps the most unfamiliar term of the five is *percolating*. The authors use it instead of *prewriting*. Percolating prepares writers to write. They talk to friends about their ideas, mentally rehearse lines, read, lie on the couch or stare out the window and think. Idea and image incubate in the writer. Mayher and his colleagues eschew the term *prewriting* because it implies that these activities take place only before the first draft is begun.

Percolating, by contrast, occurs during the entire writing process. Writers percolate when they sit back from their drafts and reread and consider their words and thinking. Writers percolate when they read more about their subject or seek out someone for further talk. In addition, writers also percolate when they leave their writing desk. I do some of my best percolating when I'm in the swimming pool, lapping the meters in steady rhythm. Percolating also occurs, I suspect,

when writers are not actively thinking about the writing—
when ideas, problems, and images are left to work in the rich
compost of the subconscious.

"Percolating," write Mayher, Lester, and Pradl, "involves
everything that happens to the writer apart from the actual
setting of marks on paper" (5). I would like to expand their
definition of this well-named and useful concept to include
certain kinds of marking on paper. Under percolating might
also come brainstorming and mapping activities that generate
ideas and information, the drawing of diagrams or pictures,
the jotting of notes, impressions, or trial lines—in short,
anything done in relation to the piece of writing aside from
producing a draft or revising one.

Drafting means getting a vision down on paper, cutting loose
with it, so to speak, with little regard to refinement and
correctness, but much regard to making meaning. The important thing in the drafting stage is to get words on paper—
not necessarily the right words, but the first words. If descriptions are not fully rendered, if thinking is half-baked, if
assertions are unconnected, that's fine. That's what a draft is
for. When we learn to interact with our drafts, they tell us
what needs to be expanded, refined, or expunged.

Matters of clarity, emotional payoffs, precise word selection,
and fully developed, connected thinking are most often addressed during the *revising* stage. Writing is not live television.
Writers can see their words again and again, can play with
them and create new ones until the writing rings true. And
the re-seeing will be clearer and sharper if the writer has the
benefit of other pairs of eyes, if she gets response from real
readers during the process of writing. In the case of students,
those real readers should be their peers as well as their teachers.

"I think it helps to have someone your own age read your
writing," wrote Karen, a sophomore. "They understand better
what you're trying to say, and they make good suggestions
that maybe an adult wouldn't have thought of."

The *editing* and *publishing* stages of a writing process should
arrive holding hands. To edit something that has no chance
of publication wastes a writer's time; to publish something
that hasn't been edited invites readers to dismiss a writer's
words. Editing is necessary only when writers have said what
they intended (or learned to intend) and are now ready to
publish the writing in some way.

When writers are ready to publish, they want to present their audience the cleanest copy possible. They want spelling, punctuation, usage, and grammar to be standard in most instances. When variations from the standard occur, they do because writers are using them to serve their stylistic purposes. Any accidents of written discourse have been corrected. This is not mere courtesy. It is shrewd psychology. Peter Elbow has called all the rules and conventions of correctness "writing's surface" (1981, 168). It should be smooth, unrippled, unnoticed. Writers want nothing distracting readers from the meanings that lie in the depths of the writing.

Publishing, Mayher and colleagues explain, means "any public presentation" (6). Students must write for more than a teacher, pen in hand, hunched over a desk ready to cast judgment. Sharing their writing with others motivates students and teaches them that writing is a vibrant part of society. For students, publishing includes posting the writing on the bulletin board; sharing it with the class; performing or orally interpreting it during a school assembly; having it printed in a school or commercial anthology, newspaper, or magazine.

A writing process model I have adapted from the terms of Mayher et al. is shown in Figure 4–2. Because I believe with Mayher and his colleagues that percolating takes place throughout the writing process, I have included a *predrafting* stage in my model. This provides a place for those percolating

FIGURE 4–2

activities that occur before a draft is begun. I have progressively reduced the size of *percolating*, for its role diminishes the closer a writer gets to publication.

All along the process it is imperative that the teacher-crafter demonstrates to apprentices all the stages of the writing process. Teachers cannot merely preach process writing; they must do process writing and show that doing to students. Such practice creates clarity of purpose for everyone. It also develops mutual respect between teacher and students.

Undergirding every step of the writing process is plenty of teacher and peer response. When students share their writing amid the stages of its creation, they find out how their ideas strike others, what questions their words elicit from readers. My process model leads up, not down, to publishing, because carrying a piece to publication is a triumph, a celebration.

REFERENCES

Calkins, Lucy McCormick. 1986. *The Art of Teaching Writing*. Portsmouth, NH: Heinemann.

Elbow, Peter. 1981. *Writing with Power*. New York: Oxford University Press.

Mayher, John S.; Lester, Nancy; and Pradl, Gordon M. 1983. *Learning to Write/Writing to Learn*. Upper Montclair, NJ: Boynton/Cook.

Writing Processes
in One High-School Classroom

The best writing processes are flexible and organic. They bend and grow to meet a writer's needs. Teaching processes, too, are ideal when they are flexible and organic enough to meet the students' needs, and the teacher's. I heard a teacher say once, "In the classroom you can only do what you're comfortable with."

I agree with that, although some teachers have used a like philosophy to justify a slide into stubborn stagnation. Such teachers remain righteously ignorant of the latest thinking in their field. They refuse to try anything new because they may initially be uncomfortable with it. They cease trying to grow. And the profession is the worse for it.

I understand, though, that secondary English teachers' classrooms will reflect their personalities, histories, philosophies of education, knowledge of writing, commitment, and understanding of teenagers. Know me and you know my classroom. The following discussion represents how writing processes operate with students in one classroom—mine.

PREDRAFTING

I make assignments broad enough for students to stretch and find their own places, their own topics, their own approaches. I often assign something specific, such as a childhood remembrance, a persuasive piece, free-verse poetry, a character sketch, a satire, or a literary paper. Sometimes I assign simply a piece of writing. With some sophomores recently within a curriculum designed to allow a lot of writing time, I began the course by reading a letter I had written them. In it I told them we would be writing in class during the next twelve weeks, that they were free to write what they wanted. The only requirement was that they must write. Then we went to work at the craft of writing.

But usually I make more specific assignments, and when I do, some students are compelled from within to write something else. Most of the time I have no objections. A character sketch takes on the proportions of a short story. A literary paper becomes a satire. A narrative is compressed and pared to a poem.

Whatever the assignment, I allow two to four days before a draft must be created, although students may, of course, write anytime they're ready. During this predrafting time, we percolate. We think and look at possibilities—examples of writing in the genre I'm asking students to try.

Occasionally, I'll show students the writing of professionals, especially if we're trying a more difficult genre, such as satire. In literature and current magazines and newspapers I can find a wide variety of examples to share. But most of the writing we read and discuss has been written by students from years past. This is important. Students need to see that others their age have traveled this way before them, have created meaningful writing out of the stuff of their lives. My colleagues and I have no trouble finding student writing. For years now our high school has published *Menagerie*, an annual creative-arts anthology loaded with poetry, various genres of prose, and artwork.

I also keep a file of good student writing. Most of the pieces in it were written by students in my own classes. Some were written by students from afar, and I happened to find them in my reading. By "good writing" I mean "writing that works" (Provost 1980, 9–10). Usually, such writing shows rather than tells, delivers specific information, employs strong verbs, makes a point, and is driven by a distinctive voice.

I prescribe no form for students. No five-paragraph essays. No sketches that begin with a physical description of the character. No pseudo-poems that follow some formula, such as placing a noun on line one, writing three lines that contain present participles, and concluding with a line that repeats the noun. No. My purpose is not to corral students, but to throw open the gate.

The samples of writing I share have succeeded with the assignment in different ways. I'm not looking for students to choose one of those ways, although they may. What I really want them to see is that they may try anything. Possibilities, both in approach and subject matter, abound.

While we're in the midst of the predrafting stage, reading and discussing what works in the examples of student writing, we also write. We try brainstorming, mapping, or other discovery exercises to begin generating ideas. Before drafting a character piece, sophomore Dwayne placed his subject in the middle of a sheet of paper and quickly mapped out what he knew and could jog himself to remember about his cousin Charlie (Figure 5–1).

Over a semester I demonstrate and have students try a variety of ways for discovering viable topics. When students are readying themselves to write a childhood remembrance, for example, I have them write what James Moffett calls "a spontaneous memory monologue" (1981, 40).

The idea is to look around the room until you see something that raises a memory. Then begin writing. Follow that memory only until your words make you think of another. Then go with the new memory until. . . . The idea is to skip around, uncritically pulling memories from your subconscious, ac-

FIGURE 5–1

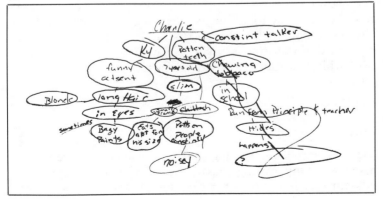

cumulating as many as possible in fifteen or twenty minutes.
The writer takes a wondrous voyage.

One student wrote this after he saw a picture of Bob Dylan
laminated to a piece of wood, hanging above my chalkboard:

> We made plaques in Bible School too, I remember the
> first time we came to this church I didn't know any
> body but things have changed know. I remember our
> other house and how dad was alway buying old trucks,
> putting bonds on them and getting them ready to paint.
> then he would sell them, get another and start all over.
> then we bought Grandpa's old '47 Willy's jeep holes in
> the top the old blue paint peeling off old skinny tires,
> cob webs all over. I remember when it was running,
> Great Grandpa came over and we all went for a ride. We
> have had a lot of fun in the old jeep. I remember
> Grandpa's farm back the lane, making apple cider. We
> would make about fourty to fifty gallons a day. (We had
> a lot of help) Grandpa lives in Floridia Know and I
> don't hardly see him but once or twice a year. The last
> time we went down there was in '72 it was beautiful, life
> on the beach. I think its about time to go down there
> again.
>
> *Craig Theobald, sophomore*

We also talk over our ideas during this time of percolation.
Craig read his memory voyage to a small group of peers who
then reported to him what they found interesting as readers.
Because of the group's inquiries, Craig did further talking
about some of the topics he had generated. He divulged more
information about his church, the Willys jeep, and Florida.
He ended up writing a vivid narrative about cider-making
day, which included a vivid characterization of his great-
grandpa.

DRAFTING

I've been enrolled in writing courses in which we writers never
wrote anything during class time. The teacher apparently
thought that students weren't learning to write unless he, the

teacher, was talking about writing. People rarely learn to write that way. They learn to write when they are writing—producing words, working with words, seeing what they say, asking themselves questions, and making choices based upon that seeing and questioning.

Using class time to write in secondary schools is essential. When students write during class, teachers can be sure that they all engage in a sustained act of writing, that all experience the fulfillment, excitement, and magic of a text being generated under their hands. During class time in other craft disciplines, students make music, paintings, sculptures, garments, cabinets. In writing class they should make writing.

Therefore, I seek to establish in my classroom a "studio atmosphere," as Graves calls it (1983, 13), a place conducive to making writing. Noise level and movement will vary, depending upon what students are doing. . . .

Terry enters the room; the tardy bell rings a split second later. He's been out in the hall, talking to his girlfriend. He's walking like a boy who's just been kissed. He takes his seat and joins the heated discussion about a crucial penalty in last night's televised football game.

Four girls in the front right corner of the room, glad to see each other, tell of their day's unbelievable trials. Their eyes grow wide, their mouths drop open. They laugh. David sits sullenly in the farthest corner of the room. His disdainful expression is a permanent fixture. Amy, quiet as usual, listens to three students nearby complain animatedly about Mr. Bock, a social-studies teacher. On the opposite side of the room, Cheryl stands by Eric's desk. They talk, smile, then she heads across the room to her seat by two girls who share other classes with her. Despite David's sullenness, a friendly hubbub prevails.

Today I've set aside the entire period to get a draft on paper. For the last three days plus a weekend, we've explored and talked and thought about what we might write. Today we write a draft, produce a chunk of writing that will be like a lifeboat: with it we'll be able to get where we need to go.

"Class," I say, "find your spots." I've talked about each of them finding that special place in the room where they are safe and comfortable, where they "feel naturally happy and strong" (Castaneda 1968, 19), a place where they can write well. Their spot.

Students begin to move about the classroom.

"I'm going to turn out the harsh fluorescent lights," I say. "Make the room more intimate. The daylight streaming through the windows will illuminate your desk tops." I don't douse the lights every time we draft, but today it seems right.

Terry moves his desk so it faces a wall. Cheryl and her friends seek out the piece of carpet in the right front corner of the room. They lie on their stomachs, writing pads before them. Three or four other students move their desks closer to the windows where the light is better.

"Hey, Mr. Romano," says Zack, "can I move these papers off this desk?"

"No, that's my stuff. I'm going to sit there."

"How come you're gonna sit here?"

"That's my spot."

Zack stands there, holding a pencil in one hand and three sheets of borrowed paper in the other, looking about the room for a spot.

I put a cassette into the portable tape player I've brought from home.

"What'd you bring?" asks Greg. "Something we can jam to?"

"No," I say, "something we can write to."

"I'm going into the hall," says Vicky.

I nod acknowledgment as she pulls her desk through the door.

Bonnie and Kristi, two of the best writers in class, have written passes to the library, where they like to work. I sign them and they're on their way. "May the Muse be with you," I call after them.

"She's always with me," says Bonnie, glancing over her shoulder, smiling. She and Kristi walk to the door, past Mark and Tony who sit on the floor, their backs against the wall.

I survey the room to see where others have found their spots. Three are sitting at the table along a side wall of the room. John has found himself a cubbyhole between a metal storage cabinet and book stand. Zack has seated himself at my desk. Some students haven't moved their seats an inch, opting to keep them aligned in rows.

I punch play on the cassette player, and barely audible, low-key, instrumental jazz becomes part of the background.

I flick off the lights and weave through the room to see if anyone has a question or query I can settle.

"How long does this have to be?" I hear as I pass one student's desk.

"Long enough," I answer sincerely.

He looks instantly exasperated, has missed my sincerity.

"I don't mean that as a wisecrack," I say. "Some writing works with half a page. Other writing needs hundreds of pages. Be honest and take a shot. Carry the piece through to the end without shortcuts. Then the draft will be long enough."

I head to the desk where I left my paper and pens. Around the room in the half-light, most students have begun writing. Every now and then I look up from my own work to check out the room. I see Cheryl on the carpet lean over to her friend, whisper something. The friend looks at Cheryl's paper, whispers something back. Cheryl asks a further question. The friend responds briefly. Cheryl nods and now both are writing again.

Absolute quiet is not a must to the classroom writing workshop, though when students are drafting, the room is quieter than during other activities. I insist upon this. I want each writer to have the opportunity to cultivate the inner atmosphere necessary for getting words on paper. That means limited talking. This rule has little to do with silence and everything to do with reducing interruptions. I don't know what the atmosphere of each of my students' home life is like. I do know that for many the school day is packed with classes. Sometimes the study hall is a carnival. In my classroom, at least, I want to ensure that my students have extended time to concentrate fully on creating a draft. Students who are idly talking fail to begin that concentration. Worse, they disrupt the concentration of others. Much talking will come on other days, when it is an essential part of the writing process.

Ten minutes into the period, I rise from my seat to talk to Jodi. My periodic glances have told me she hasn't written much. I stoop by her desk.

"The words coming tough?"

Her mouth is tense. "I know what I want to write. I just don't know how to start."

"Oh," I say with lightness, "don't let that stop you."

"But beginnings are important."

"You bet they are. They're crucial. But you can always fashion a new beginning after you see where the draft goes."

Jodi looks skeptical.

"I do that all the time," I add. "I rarely end up going with the first words I put down."

"I'm afraid I'll get it all wrong and it won't go anywhere."

"It'll go somewhere. Don't be too critical in the beginning. Just accept what comes into your mind on the subject—a word, a bit of dialog, an emotion, anything really—and then put it down." I glance at her clean white paper and the pen she holds in her hand. Those ten minutes must have been brutal. "There's nothing like getting some specific words down to knock you loose."

"I'll try."

I leave Jodi's desk and head back to my own. By the time I'm seated, she's writing.

When the period ends, most students have produced a substantial piece of writing, and some ask to keep their drafts overnight to finish. Naturally, I let them. I keep in mind that some students have already formed their own productive writing habits, however alien they seem to me.

"I like to write at my desk in my room with the radio fairly loud playing some Zeppelin or Hank Williams, Jr.," a student once explained to me. "The music is a constant noise I can count on the entire time I'm writing, instead of listening to my family and three televisions on three different stations."

REVISING

Near the end of a drafting day, I sometimes circulate about the room, holding brief chats with some of the students, just long enough to find out what they have written and where they think they're headed. Sometime during the next couple of days, I have students meet in small peer writing groups or with partners to read their work aloud. I want them to help each other learn where their writing is working and where it isn't.

Before they meet in peer response groups, I make sure I demonstrate how one might work.

"Bonnie, Eric, Tony, and Cheryl," I call out, "take these seats up here in the front of the room and make a semicircle facing me." I have chosen these students because their requisite load of adolescent self-consciousness appears minimal. They won't be too shy to speak their thoughts while their peers observe.

"These four are my response group," I explain. "I have a first draft of something I've written, and I need to begin understanding how it hits other people. We have the perfect opportunity for that, since we're all gathered together for the common purpose of writing."

I pause. Everyone is attentive; we've just crossed over into new territory that will become part of our work routine.

"What I want you guys to do," I say, turning to the four I've selected, "is to listen as I read. Bear down hard to hear my words. When I've finished I want you to simply report to me what you heard. You don't have to say you liked something or didn't like something. Just tell me what you remember, what stuck with you. That will help. And then ask me some real questions that the writing has raised in your mind."

I turn to the class. "My purpose is twofold: One, I'm really curious to learn what these readers respond to and don't respond to. That may help me later when I revise. Two, I want them to get me talking further about my subject. Talking about it will make me think more about it."

My draft is titled "Third Strike." I sit down at a desk and give the piece the best oral reading I can. I finish and wait. Silence. My group needs to be nudged.

"What got through? What can you tell me?"

More silence; then, "I remember you saying the kids' names a lot—Kenny, Steve, and the two others."

"Me too."

I nod. Silence. "Anything else?"

"Those boys you mentioned always struck out."

"Yeah, I remember the word *nip*. It's good."

"Yes," I say. "I like how it describes what it's like to barely foul-tip a softball."

"I liked at the end where you said *blazing grounders* and *towering home runs*."

"And *crisp line drives*," adds Eric.

"You called one group of boys 'the sluggers.'"

I nod and there is silence again. "How about questions? Any questions?"

Bonnie clears her throat. "What exactly did you mean by 'calling third strikes'?"

"Well, that's important," I say. "I've got to make sure a reader gets that. What happened was that Kenny and the three others struck out so much they always ended a big inning. So the sluggers began to call, or claim . . . maybe *claim*'s more accurate. The sluggers claimed those four boys' third strikes. So if Kenny didn't get a hit on his first two swings, then he didn't get his third strike. A slugger took it over and hit the ball for him."

"I'd have never let those guys do that," says Eric.

"They got away with it," I say. "They were tougher than most of the other boys."

"So that's why you described how Kenny and them got so nervous when they batted?"

"Partly. The other thing is they didn't want to be humiliated by having their third strike claimed. After I wrote this, I thought about how much we looked forward to recess. But I'll bet the closer the minute hand moved to dismissal the more anxious Kenny and the others got."

"If you call one group the sluggers," says Cheryl, "maybe you ought to call the other boys something."

"Didn't I call them 'the weak hitters' once or twice?"

"I didn't hear it."

"I think you did."

"Well, I can check that and see if I need to do anything."

I end the response session there. "Thank you," I tell the four who cooperated, then speak to the entire class. "When you listen to others respond to your writing, be accepting. Don't argue. Remember, your purpose is to discover what they thought and felt and to do some additional talking about your topic."

I might demonstrate small-group conferences once or twice more, again handpicking a group, but this time having a willing student share writing instead of me. I keep reinforcing the idea that to help another writer, you don't have to be critical in the way that most teenagers think of the word. You don't have to tear down. You don't have to cast judgment. Fellow writers can help a good deal by just reporting honestly how the words affected them and asking questions that coax the writer to be expansive in her talk.

Soon after these demonstrations, I get students to share their writing in peer response groups composed of from three to five members. I have no set way of establishing these groups, because I don't know of one foolproof way to make them work. At times I've carefully chosen peer groups, putting together students of varying abilities. I've put talkative students with taciturn ones. I've arranged groups so they contained equal numbers of boys and girls. I've let students choose their own groups. I've even formed groups using a combination of these ways.

No matter how the peer response groups are formed, some will work winningly, some competently, some adequately, some poorly. So I do not form peer groups in any single way. I consider individual personalities and class personality, then I go with my best instincts. The junior and senior combined class I'm teaching now I have let form their own groups. The sophomore class I'm teaching, however, I've formed into groups, spreading around the smaller number of boys, matching compatible personalities.

When students meet in their groups, I circulate around the classroom, listening in, monitoring progress, occasionally offering advice that may help a group interact more productively.

Peer response groups cause me the most unease. It's the clearest indication that I've relinquished some control, that I'm trusting teenagers more to give and take what they need. A good part of my unease stems from my excessively high expectations for how peer groups should work. I have too much of that old ideal of teaching left in me: I ran the show, cracked the whip, acted upon the students, ever fearful that they might not be working if I didn't ride herd. Even I couldn't function in the ideal peer response group I have in my head.

I look around the room and see six separate groups, plenty of teenagers jabbering away. Some of the groups are working better than others, but all the groups are working better than I think. They accomplish things that would be difficult to measure with a standardized test. Those things are important enough for me to keep peer group response as an integral part of my writing class.

I want students talking plenty about their writing. If they talk only with me, they'll fall far short of that goal. The groups give more individuals chances to become active learners, talking about their own writing and their peers'. By its very nature, conversation requires students to focus and clarify their thinking.

I also know that talking in peer response groups—without the teacher present—gives students opportunities to be more freewheeling in their conversation, so they will more readily speak the tentative idea, say the irreverent phrase, reveal a lack of knowledge, attempt to communicate the emotion they only dimly realize they feel. Most students will risk saying more among their peers than with me. And, of course, the students can learn from each other in this close contact. So I live with my discomfort and let teenagers meet in groups.

Even so, some days I change the format of peer response to let students experience another way of getting feedback. I have them read each other's drafts silently and respond in writing. For example, one time I might ask them to address some specific points:

1. Describe two strong parts of the piece.
2. Quote the most effective sentence.
3. Name one spot that you would like to see vivified.
4. Ask a question.

The students read during the entire fifty-minute period, enough time to respond to three or four drafts. At period's end they deliver their responses to the authors.

This written response is a good variation for getting help to writers. But I never abandon peer groups. The talk is too important. And so, too, is the act of reading aloud words committed to paper. An even-paced oral reading causes students to say what's on the page, something we can't assume they will always do when they read their work silently. By reading aloud, students also begin to really *hear* the sounds and rhythms of their voices, a crucial skill for writers. I want them to develop the skill of truly hearing their words. One day I want students to hear their written language when they read silently.

Sophomore Tracy tells me of another benefit of reading aloud to a small audience: "My story about how hard it is to be a cheerleader was long—I wanted everything to get in. I *thought* maybe it was too long but hoped it wasn't. The more I read, the more bored they got. Finally, I just started skipping parts."

"Did the group say anything about the piece being too long or boring?" I ask.

"They didn't have to," says Tracy. "I could feel it."

The experience made Tracy think about the essence of her essay about cheerleading. She revised, cutting out a large section on the rigors of cheerleading camp, and focusing upon a cheerleader's duties during the school year.

I do not *require* revision, but all our movement in writing class is toward working with words, shaping language, discovering vision, and clarifying it for readers. I provide class time for students to do these things. "Good writing," writes John Ciardi, "is rewriting" (1966, 149). He doesn't mean simply recopying language. He means re-evaluating, re-thinking, re-valuing, re-generating, re-creating. Revision.

I demonstrate how one writer goes about revising a piece of writing. I do this in two ways. Students need to experience both. On the overhead I put excerpts from writing I've done. If possible, I use subsequent drafts of the piece I read when we demonstrated how a peer response group could work. Students see how my words, information, and focus transformed over the course of several drafts. I ask them why they believe I made some of my revision decisions, and I also tell them my "whys"—why I cut a paragraph or created a new lead, why I broke down a complicated sentence into two or three, why I needed to add new paragraphs and then develop the change in focus, why I used a short sentence at the end of the piece. The list goes on. A teacher who writes will eventually grapple with every revision problem. I want students to see that words on paper can be crafted, that a writer has options, makes choices, solves problems.

Teachers often exhort students to revise their writing but never show them how it's done. Young writers can also benefit from seeing revision happen before their eyes. To accomplish this, I occasionally make a transparency of a piece of first-draft writing and work with it on the overhead projector. I want students to actually see me crossing out weak or imprecise words and choosing new ones, deleting whole lines and passages, asking myself questions, circling paragraphs and indicating with arrows how they might be rearranged, making plans, adding further information.

When students are working with drafts, I have my most

important conferences with them. I read or listen to their writing not as teacher-corrector, but as teacher-reader, one who always looks to be moved by writing. My intent in these conferences is to precipitate further interaction between writers and their words. This interaction, writes Calkins, is "the cutting edge of writing" (1986, 20). This edge is where a word user is honed into a writer.

I ask students how they feel about the writing. I indicate places where I thought their words worked. I ask questions that arose in me as I experienced their words. My responses are dictated by the students' responses and by what their body, eyes, and tone tell me. If a student seems ready to handle them, I make suggestions.

From my input, their peers', and their own rethinking of the text, students begin revising their drafts. I move about the classroom, seeking out those I should talk to first. Mark has had trouble getting his writing off the ground, has barely drafted a paragraph. Bonnie believes the Muse has forsaken her. At the bottom of her paper she's written, "I hate this!!!"

As I do my work, students do theirs. They reread their pieces, strike passages, and clarify sections, amending, drafting anew, rewording. After fifteen or twenty minutes of fairly silent work, the classroom takes on a hive sound, a hum as students begin conferring with each other, handing over their papers or reading aloud, testing their revisions on individual readers they trust.

This personal student-to-student dialog is important. Students need to find out whom among their peers they can comfortably and profitably get help from. Adult writers do the same. I have colleagues and friends I like and respect, but I don't ask all of them for response to my writing. I choose my responders carefully. Some I am comfortable talking freely with and listening to, some I am not.

Marla, a senior, tells me about her best respondent. "First Mom reads my writing to herself. Next, I read it to her so she can hear how it sounds in my voice, then she makes comments that help me improve it."

As I leave one student's side after a conference, I scan the room. Some are working in duos, some in impromptu peer groups. Others work alone. My students are engaged with language. And I feel good as they all work toward a revised draft.

How many revisions do students do? That depends on the piece of writing, the students, and their intentions. Some pieces call for no revision. They may be completed. Or they may be going nowhere and the students know it, so they leave the piece and draft something new. Usually, though, a piece is revised once or twice.

I'm working with students the whole way; our conferences help them see what may be done. Gradually, as students learn to become their own readers, they see possibilities themselves. Sometimes I nudge students, sometimes I push. Sometimes I back off. Occasionally, when a piece of writing is really hot, when it's going somewhere and the student feels the thrill of it, three or four revisions are not abnormal.

EDITING

When students believe they are finished with the shape and content of a piece of writing, we spend a class period or two correcting errors of spelling, punctuation, grammar, and usage. Occasionally, I teach a minilesson to the entire class about some particular writing convention, but this is rare. Most often I ask students to reread my response to the last piece of writing they carried through to publication. On it I noted one or two errors of editing convention the student made repeatedly, errors important enough to address next in learning to produce standard written English.

The student then works to eradicate that particular error on the about-to-be-published piece of writing. I help; the students help each other. Many of them, after all, have no problem with such things as apostrophes, sentence sense, or dialect-related usage errors. When dealing with teenagers who have spelling problems, I employ a strategy that Donald Graves has used successfully with elementary-school children (1983, 193). I ask students to first pick out words they have a hunch might be spelled wrong. From this basis of self-diagnosis, we then check and correct spelling, trying, when appropriate, to learn the spelling of some words or a rule that would be useful.

Many elementary-school students keep track of the editing skills they are working to learn. My students do this too. They keep every scrap of their writing in folders or three-ring notebooks. Somewhere, often on the back front cover, they list their editing bugaboos, the errors they have been most prone to. When they are ready to edit a new piece, they begin by consulting this list.

Editing skills are important, an indispensable part of the process of creating finished writing. Errors of written convention stick out and are easily detected, it seems, by everyone except the writer who makes them. Many readers, including teachers, mistakenly (or conveniently) dismiss the content of a poorly edited piece. Some readers even foolishly judge writers' seriousness and intelligence by the accuracy of their spelling.

"I know I shouldn't," a school board member once said to me, "but when I see a spelling error on a letter or report, I'm immediately turned off."

Correctness is of little importance to readers when they are reading flawlessly edited copy. Let them spot one editing error, however, and suddenly correctness is all-important. Surely, we must work to educate the public and our colleagues to be reasonable about editing errors. And we must also work to help our students master more editing skills. What we mustn't do, though, is panic. We must strive to keep editing skills in perspective—a part of the writing process. Countless people have had their attitudes about the creative act of writing permanently darkened by a teacher who emphasized perfection in editing to the point that all other parts of the writing process did not matter.

Several years ago, Bill Melloh, a physical-education teacher, volunteered to handle the coffee fund at my school, a move to meet the needs of the staff "caffiends," as he called them, simply and efficiently. His occasional memos make for good reading and are full of voice, humor, and pertinent information.

"I like your memos so much," I said to Bill. "I was wondering what kind of writing experience you had in school."

Bill's upper lip curled. His nostrils flared, and he snarled, "The bitch gave me an F if I had one comma fault."

Recently, I dined with a former high-school classmate, now a successful businessman. When we discussed my work teaching writing to high-school students, he said apologetically, "I was never very good at writing. I could never get the punctuation in the right place."

Nancie Atwell of Boothbay Harbor, Maine, remarks that whenever strangers find out she's an English teacher they immediately say, "Oh. Then I guess I'd better watch my grammar" (1985, 147).

Our profession has become synonymous with fastidiousness. And I don't like it. Spelling, usage, grammar, punctuation—editing skills—are part of a piece of writing, along with organization, diction, clarity, voice, style, and quality of information. Expert editing cannot make insipid writing vibrant, nor does less-than-perfect editing negate powerful thought and language.

Young writers are learners in *all* aspects of the writing craft. It is patently false to send them the message that growth in writing depends mainly upon the ability to produce perfectly edited copy. Mastery of editing skills will not ensure the production of high-quality writing. I've read too many samples of writing from government officials, lawyers, and school and hospital administrators that were wordy, pompous, vague, mealymouthed, and perfectly edited.

PUBLISHING

English classes are often sedate places when it comes to student writing. Students hand in papers; teachers comment upon them, hand them back, move on to the next assignment. There is no passion, no triumphant celebration of success and accomplishment. The sad part is that when students work at writing as process, they succeed in hundreds of ways—all worthy and significant, all deserving of sharing and celebrating.

The most triumphant moment in education I've ever witnessed occurred when I visited the classroom of my art-teacher colleague, Kai Bailey. One of her students sat at the potter's wheel for the first time. Grouped in front of the girl were more than a dozen students, anxiously watching. Kai urged the girl to take hold of the madly spinning clay. She did, tentatively, and the clay bounced and jolted her arms.

"You can't be afraid of it," said Kai. "You're the potter. You're the artist."

The girl tried, but still the wheel and material mastered her. She kept at it, though, trying to gain control of the clay, while the wheel hummed, Kai gently coached, and all those other students stood by, close to deciding yea or nay about pottery making. And suddenly the girl centered the clay. It spun wetly and smoothly in her hands, magically responsive to her touch, the wonderfully muddy water seeping between her fingers.

The girl's eyes shined in triumph. The students glanced at each other, at ease. Kai, who'd witnessed hundreds of such scenes, smiled broadly with giddy excitement for this girl who had learned so dramatically. Me? My eyes, too, shined. The hair on my arms stood up. I was astonished and happy and exhilarated and . . . envious. Why, I wondered, couldn't my students experience such triumphs when they have succeeded in their writing?

They can. Through publishing, the triumphs that occur quietly in writers' minds and are subsequently put on paper can be celebrated. After hard, successful work at writing, students must have a chance to share without criticism those struggled-over words with an audience. Occasionally, we print the students' writing in some way—in a photocopied classroom collection, the school newspaper, or a creative arts anthology. But the kind of publication that most often occurs in my class is an oral sharing of the work. I have a stool in the front of the room—an author's stool, if you will—which each student and I sit upon when we share finished writing (Graves and Hansen, 1983).

If a student indicates great shyness, I offer to read for him. If a student has written a piece so personal that he doesn't want it public, I don't require him to share. But these occasions are infrequent. As students get more experience reading work in progress in small groups, as the entire class grows into a support community, the shy students read and the emotion-packed stories are shared.

Most students enjoy sharing, though few let that be seen. They have gone through a process in shaping their language. And through this process they've created work they are proud of. When they read aloud their final pieces, writing becomes public and social—human voices speak and reach out. Sometimes class members respond with appropriate laughter or brief comments of praise. And sometimes they sit respectfully silent. Written words move people in many ways.

REFERENCES

Atwell, Nancie. 1985. "Writing and Reading from the Inside Out." In *Breaking Ground: Teachers Relate Reading and Writing in the Elementary School*, edited by Jane Hansen, Thomas Newkirk, and Donald Graves. Portsmouth, NH: Heinemann.

Calkins, Lucy McCormick. 1986. *The Art of Teaching Writing*. Portsmouth, NH: Heinemann.

Castaneda, Carlos. 1968. *The Teachings of Don Juan: A Yaqui Way of Knowledge*. New York: Ballantine Books.

Ciardi, John. 1966. "One Writer's Work Habits." In *On Writing by Writers*, edited by William W. West. Boston: Ginn and Co.

Graves, Donald H. 1983. *Writing: Teachers & Children at Work*. Portsmouth, NH: Heinemann.

Graves, Donald H., and Hansen, Jane. 1983. "The Author's Chair." *Language Arts* 60 (February):176–83.

Moffett, James. 1981. *Active Voice: A Writing Program Across the Curriculum*. Upper Montclair, NJ: Boynton/Cook.

Provost, Gary. 1980. *Make Every Word Count*. Cincinnati, OH: Writer's Digest Books.

CHAPTER

Writing Processes in Perspective:
A Dialog

The scene is the teachers' workroom in a typical high school. One teacher is seated at a table and has just begun to write when an excited colleague bursts through the doorway. . . .

At last I have the writing process straight!

The process, huh?

Yes, I've got it down pat.

I'm glad to hear that.

I have it figured out precisely.

That's impressive.

Let me demonstrate. How long have you been sitting here writing?

I just sat down.

This is *too* easy!

What do you mean?

If you just sat down, then you're definitely prewriting.

Well. . . .

Wait a minute. This stuff on the page doesn't look like prewriting at all. It looks like you're . . . are you drafting?

Well, kind of. But I don't know everything I might say yet.

Then maybe you'd better get back to basics.

What basics are you talking about? You're not one of those people who still believes you can teach writing by having students perform grammar and usage exercises?

Certainly not! This is a modern writing teacher you're talking to.

79

I guess that's good.

Of course it is. Now, the basic I'm referring to is prewriting. Do some planning before you make a draft.

I'm planning now.

How can that be? You said you were drafting now.

I am. I'm planning while I'm drafting.

Why, that's preposterous. You simply can't do that.

I can't?

No, you can't mix prewriting and drafting. You have to be doing one or the other. Get with the process, man!

But as you can see, I'm both planning and drafting, prewriting and writing.

Don't be absurd! I suppose next you're going to tell me you can do prewriting *after* you've started writing.

Yes, I do some of my best planning after I've produced a chunk of writing.

Then why call it prewriting?

I don't. I call it percolating.

Percolating? You mean like coffee?

Kind of. You know, ideas, images, thoughts, insights, connections, impressions—all bubbling through my consciousness and some of it fermenting in my subconscious.

But what about prewriting?

The word *prewriting* was a good way to label and explain a part of creating writing that had long been neglected by teachers, usually those who did little writing themselves.

You mean *prewriting* doesn't apply anymore?

Sure it does.

Thank God!

Thank Murray.

Murray who?

Never mind, I'll tell you later. It's a big subject.

Listen, I've got a real dilemma now. How should I deal with prewriting in my classroom?

The same way you must deal with every aspect of writing.

Come on, don't give me riddles. I've got to face scores of students tomorrow. What are you talking about?

Be sensible.

Can you be more specific?

Writing is not a goose-step activity. Don't make inflexible rules out of writing-process categories.

Oh, don't worry. I wouldn't do that.

Good. A lot of abuse has been meted out to students in the name of the writing process.

Abuse? Like what?

Like this: I knew a teacher once who received a knockout essay from a student who'd written the entire piece at home the night before.

Bet he was glad to get that.

He didn't know whether he was or not.

Huh?

He wasn't sure.

I thought you said the essay was a knockout.

Oh, it was. The writing was excellent, but the teacher experienced acute conflict of process pedagogy.

Acute what?

Acute conflict of process pedagogy.

Could you explain that?

Well, see, the student said that the previous evening, while thinking about doing some social-studies homework, she suddenly understood what was wrong with the dress-code policy at school. She immediately went up to her room, wrote a draft, read it to her sister to get some response from her, revised a few spots, corrected some errors, then typed a final copy.

Wow! What motivation!

The piece wound up in the next issue of the school newspaper.

An A performance for sure!

Well, no.

What? How come?

Because of that acute conflict of process pedagogy I mentioned.

Huh?

See, the kid had drafted, revised, edited, and published, but she hadn't done any prewriting. Therefore, her teacher determined, she had not gone entirely through the writing process. She'd done only four-fifths of it, barely meeting the state standards for minimum competency.

So what grade did the teacher give her?

He gave her a C+.

A C+! For a dynamite response to something that directly affected her? For a piece of writing so hot and timely that it went right into the school newspaper?

I'm afraid so.

Unbelievable. A stinking C+.

Yeah, I know. Here's the way the teacher figured it. Since the student had completed four-fifths of the writing process, he gave her an 80%, which is a C+ on the school grading scale.

Eighty percent. My, my.

The way the teacher explained it, the kid was lucky to get that.

What?

Yeah, English department policy required every student to do at least three revisions of a piece of writing. The girl had done only one. The teacher decided to be lenient, though, and gave her full credit for revising anyway.

But a C+! . . . Sometimes that acute conflict of process pedagogy can go hard with students.

Don't you know it.

I'll bet the kid learned she'd better prewrite next time.

That's the sad part. She already *had* prewritten.

I thought you said. . . .

She'd done all the prewriting she needed right in her head.

In her head? Oh! Percolating, right?

Right.

So was the student bitter about her experience with prewriting?

I don't know. But she had some time to think about it.

What do you mean?

That knockout essay about the inconsistencies in the school dress code got her a three-day suspension from school.

There's a lesson in education!

The profession's full of 'em.

You know, when I came in here, I was certain I at last understood the writing process. Now I'm not so sure. I mean, you sit there and say that you're percolating and drafting at the same time. Is that what you're really doing?

Well, actually, while I've been working at this, I've done some revising and polishing, too. And some editing—notice how I added another *o* at the end of that last *to*.

Oh, Lord! Now I'm really confused. Talk about conflict of process pedagogy! I suppose next you'll say that you are publishing this.

You're reading it, aren't you?

OK. I'm beginning to get the picture. Is this how the writing process works all the time?

No, it's how it's working for me this time.

You mean there isn't one writing process?

Precisely.

Ohhhhh—I'm going to be ill.

Take it easy now.

If there isn't one writing process, how will I ever make up an objective test?

You'll be all right.

Giving up Warriner's was hard enough to face, but this!

Listen—remember the final paper you fretted over in that graduate-school class?

I fret over most of my papers. Which class are you talking about—Decision-Making Vagaries in Prepubescent Males?

No, not that one. It was the class you took instead of attending the Ohio Writing Project last summer.

Oh, Literary Conundrums of Modernist and Postmodernist American Satirists.

That's the one.

Brilliant professor!

I'm sure he was. But remember your final paper?

Sure I do.

Now the process of writing that was different from the process of writing that party invitation last week, wasn't it?

Naturally.

And you know that you and I complete similar writing tasks in different ways.

Of course—we're different people.

Right! All your students are different too. And they write for different reasons. The thing to work for is that each of them develops personal writing processes that are productive.

Personal writing processes?

Yes, productive ones.

I guess I can live with that.

You'll have to.

But answer one question.

I'll try.

At the very start of this, just as you were beginning to make marks on paper when I walked into the room, were you percolating or drafting?

Oh, no. . . .

Please, you said you'd try.

OK. You honestly want to know what I was doing?

Yes.

What if the answer I give you isn't the one you want? Will you be satisfied with it?

As long as it's honest, I'll be satisfied.

OK. What I have truly been doing this whole time is thinking.

That's all?

That's everything.

7

The Crucial Role of Conferencing

Talk is essential in a writing class. Writers need to share their writing and hear others, particularly a sensitive teacher, talking about it with interest, asking genuine questions it has raised. And, just as important, writers need opportunities to talk about their own writing, to elaborate on information, discuss plans, verbalize dilemmas or problems they face. From such talk student writers begin to think critically about what they're saying and how they're saying it. In turn, when students speak, teachers learn things about them that will affect instruction. Teaching and learning will not be deaf; they will be based upon oral response, with all its potential for clear, immediate communication and the development of warm rapport.

The "Due Friday" writing-process model called for no teacher response except a terminal one—the grade, accompanied by written words justifying it. Students got back their final papers filled with thorough error accounting and teacher comments, usually penned in rage red. If a bold student requested a conference for further explanation of the teacher's response, the session usually wasn't a conference at all. It was an assault. The teacher led the charge, exposing flaws of language and logic, defeating the student with terminology or irrefutable pronouncements, possibly mentioning the chance of performing better on the next paper. The conference did little to encourage the student to write again.

But underpinning a modern writing-process model is plenty

of response from peers and teacher every step of the way, from generating ideas to editing the final paper. The teacher is a key figure. No writing class can be successful without the teacher talking to students about their work. Humane, student-centered writing conferences accomplish so much: We teachers come to understand our students far better, can help them learn to control their writing processes, and can directly teach them strategies and skills that will make them better writers. Each student becomes a somebody, the indispensable participant in a respectful one-to-one talk with a teacher. In conferences, students begin to reflect actively on their writing as they experience how their words have come through to a real reader. And, through our sensitive comments and questions, students begin to internalize ways in which they can respond to their peers.

In the Prologue of his novel *Slapstick*, Kurt Vonnegut recommends that people start treating each other with common decency (1976, 3). This advice is also the basic rule for conducting writing conferences with teenagers. There is no room for disrespect. Humanely conducted conferences begin relationships of trust, understanding, and support, which nurture and seal positive bonds between teacher and students. When such relationships develop, communication lines clear; student and teacher are receptive; learning is ready to happen for everyone.

The initial job of the teacher is to make the student feel worthy, comfortable, and accepted. The teacher's tone of voice should extend respect and courtesy, not imperiousness or condescension. The conference is not a time to offhandedly use complicated grammatical terms such as *introductory adverbial clause*, which may serve only to intimidate students and convince them they are outsiders when it comes to writing.

Even the arrangement of furniture in the conference area can either reassure or intimidate. To sit facing each other, for example, is not ideal. Such seating forces too many eye-to-eye confrontations and might make some students feel trapped. And any arrangement that features the teacher's imposing desk as a barrier between the conversers can only hinder the development of a writer-to-writer relationship. A better arrangement is a student's pulling up a chair beside the teacher, so that both can look at the reason for the conference: the student's written words (Arbur 1977, 338).

Some teachers prefer variations of this arrangement, which remove the teacher's desk from the conference altogether. Colleagues of mine have set up separate conference tables, where teacher and student may sit side by side. Others have set aside two desks in a far corner of the room. My preference is to circulate about the classroom, conducting conferences on the student's turf. I pull up an empty desk beside a student; or, in crowded classrooms, I sometimes move about towing a lightweight wooden stool I can set down anywhere. Such a conferencing technique diminishes my role as teacher-authority and casts me more as a knowledgeable helper, a persona I am comfortable with and one less threatening to the student. I also like the idea of being out among the students, where others may overhear our talk and pick up ideas or learn strategies.

Once a comfortable, reassuring atmosphere is established, the conference proceeds. How it proceeds depends upon many things: where the student is in the writing process, what her attitude is toward the work, what problem is foremost in her mind at the moment, how far she has moved or been nudged in previous conferences. The teacher must listen and take cues from the student. Opening with a broad question, such as "How's the writing going?" or "Where are you now?", enables students to bring up their primary concerns.

Much of a teacher's conference time will be spent responding to a student's written words and the problems and successes that arise from them. Many researchers recommend that a teacher's initial response give back to the writer the words, information, and ideas that got through. Peter Elbow has called this strategy "pointing" (1973, 85). By telling the writer specific things he remembered from the text, the responder, in effect, points to them. Donald Graves and Jane Hansen call the same technique "receiving" (1983, 176). The responder tells the writer what he learned and thus acknowledges its reception.

This simple retelling of what the piece was about, what words were remembered, also helps the responder recall more of the writing. Verbalizing remembered information triggers the retrieval of more information. In addition, the pointing or receiving demonstrates to the writer that she knows things and has communicated them, thus reassuring her and lifting her confidence.

I drop to one knee beside a student's desk. I read aloud a poem she's written:

SNAKIE

It slithered up and struck
when noone was looking
But is'nt that when
most bad things occur?

It slid and wrapped,
consuming chairs and tables
And the snake got them
Befor they got out.

She looks at me quizzically, her head tilted.

"This metaphor with the snake is powerful, Dawn, makes me feel how evil and sinister it is."

"A snake was the only thing I could compare it to."

"Nothing could have fit better," I say. "You know, I wondered how much I was reading into this."

"What do you mean?"

"I know what you're writing about, so I filled in details that you don't mention—I knew your mom and dad. I know your sisters."

"You mean the poem is 'private writing,' like the book says?"

"The metaphor isn't private. You could just leave this as a vivid comparison, unless you want an objective reader to feel your devastating experience."

"By filling in the details?"

"Yes."

"What do you think?"

"There's strength here, Dawn—the snake metaphor, those words *slid* and *wrapped*. Why not see where the strength leads you?"

She nods.

I am not a rapid reader. My words-per-minute rate would make a reading specialist drool to get me in front of a tachistoscope. Even so, when students are working with short pieces—brief drafts, poems, leads, revisions of lines or paragraphs—I read them and hold brief conferences with students during class. But when students have written longer prose pieces, as they often do, I find it necessary to read the drafts at home or during my preparation period so that less class time is taken up with my cold reading.

When I read drafts outside of class, I certainly don't grade them, and rarely do I write on them. My purpose in reading drafts is to discover what the students are doing so that I might help them accomplish their intentions and learn more about the writing craft. I usually write a student's name on a clean sheet of paper, read the piece, then make notes consisting of code words to help me remember, questions, and references to a particular page, paragraph, line, or word. Here is what I jotted based upon a draft in which a student sought to create a portrait of herself as a writer:

> Kim—Good stuff about reading over what you've writ-
> ten. Like to know more about "sorting out words
> before I write," it taking long time—good or bad
> habit? Leads. See some? Need good lead before
> start?

When I've finished a classroom set of student papers, I'll have about two pages filled with the students' names and my rapidly written notes. No one can decode them but me. The next day I am ready to speak to my students as an informed reader of their writing.

Teachers should not take those drafts and mark errors, point out fallacies, critique severely, and then present students with the results. Such practice should be steadfastly avoided. It can only intimidate, disillusion, and overwhelm the writers. Donald Murray (1978, 59) warns us to ease the sharply critical eye in matters of student writing, especially during the delicate growing stages when the slightest feeling of self-doubt or imagined ridicule can stunt the writing's growth, indeed kill it.

On one occasion as I read a paper with the student beside me, I absentmindedly corrected a spelling error. I glanced at the young writer, and his expression told me I had lost him. My action was irrevocable. In the student's eyes I had undergone a sudden transformation. No longer was I a reader, interested in his voice and meaning; I had become a pedant, concerned

only with correctness. There is a time to prune spelling in-
accuracies, but certainly not until most of the growing is done.

Common decency. The student is a human being, not a
mechanical writing device to be shaken like a candy machine
until the desired product pops out. If a teacher has had initial
success in cutting students loose and the students therefore
feel secure enough to write honestly, then their feelings are
real and run deep, whether they are expressed in nonstandard
usage, written with run-on sentences, or asserted with un-
supported generalizations.

Our job is to boost the self-esteem of our students. Their
errors, we must encourage them to understand, are not all-
defeating. Their writing is worthy of serious consideration.
Their voices count. The troubling emotions and experiences
they write about are not theirs alone, but part of the human
experience (Duke 1975, 45).

Dawn stands in the doorway during my conference period.
"I'm having trouble getting this started," she says.

"Let's take a look." She walks in and we sit at desks.

"I really haven't done anything more."

"Too close to it, maybe?"

"I don't know, but I want to write about it."

"It'll be tough," I say. "I wasn't able to write about my
father's death until six or seven years after it happened. Even
then I just wrote a journal entry."

"The snake comparison was easy. It's been in my head for
months. The rest is what's hard."

"You can stop if you want, Dawn, if you aren't ready.
What you've written is done well."

She is silent a moment. "What would I have to do to really
make it work?"

"What do you think readers will need in order to feel the
impact?"

"They'll need to know what happened," she says. "And
they'll need to know my parents."

I nod.

"How could I do that?" she asks.

"We've talked a lot in class about the power of vivid images.
How do you remember them that day?"

Again a brief silence; then Dawn speaks. "They were working
in the field. Mom was driving the tractor. It was a good day.

Dad was all sweaty from working, and Mom had her hair up."

"They were both working in the field, huh?"

"Yeah."

"That's a good picture. Now, just break it down to the small images, the sights and sounds."

"I can do that—I remember it."

"Will your readers need to know where they were going?"

"Isn't it clear?" She reads her words. "It isn't, not unless you already know."

"We'll know when you're through, I suspect."

A good deal of conference time is spent eliciting information from the writer, asking various questions about the writing. Jane Hansen points out that the most useful questions are those the reader genuinely needs answered (1983, 971). Such questions give writers the opportunity to clarify meaning, add further information, discover new ideas. Calkins has observed that, in the best conferences, a responder, whether teacher or peer, follows through on questions, pursuing understanding by making subsequent inquiries based upon the answer to previous questions (1983, 127).

By hearing and answering a responder's genuine questions, students learn how their vision and intent in a piece of writing can be fulfilled. And, more importantly, they gradually internalize the conference procedure, learn to conduct conferences with themselves (Calkins 1983, 138). In every class I teach, I soon discover that some students already know how to do this. I get their first drafts and I see that they have conducted extensive self-conferences, have begun to revise. They have filled margins with new writing, crossed out whole passages, recast sentences, changed or discovered their focus. They have intuitively sensed imbalances, asked themselves questions, and responded with answers. John Ciardi would applaud their writerly schizophrenia, their ability to be both "passion hot" and "critic cold" (1966, 153).

Experienced writers possess two voices. One dictates the flow of words; the second questions clarity and logic. By experiencing this questioning technique in conferences, students begin activating the second voice, begin to gain "the true freedom of the writer who looks inward rather than outward for critical evaluation" (Gutschow 1975, 100).

I cringe when a student asks, "How do you want me to write this?" or "What do you want me to do now?" All too often I have the answer, or, I should say, *an* answer. And the temptation is great to say, "Do this, this, and this." I must fight to hold back, to remain ethical, to let the writer maintain control.

At the same time, however, I want to help students. "If I know something I think will help a student," writes Murray, "I share it" (1982, 162). I do the same. I want my students to learn to control their writing processes, to make decisions on their own, and to take responsibility for them. But I also want to set up situations in which they can, as Ken Macrorie says, produce "good works" (1984, 235). I want them to experience successes, to see evidence on paper of the exciting potential that resides within them.

In the morning between classes, Dawn stops by my room, gives me a much-expanded version of her poem, and hurries to her next class. I read:

COMPENSATION

    Sweat poured off his face
    as fleks of old black hay
    clung to his bare chest and
    forearms.
    He stacked hay like a man getting
    older but with strength enough left in him.

    She had her black greying hair
    in curlers driving the tractor.
    The click and whine of
    the baler diminished all other sound

    They were happy
    We were happy.
    it had been a year since we'd
    felt that way.

    They went out that night
    and while they were drinking
    the snake appeared in another
    ballroom.

it slithered up and struck
when no one was looking.
But is'nt that when most
bad things occur?

It slid through the halls
consuming chairs and tables
noone took the bus boy
seriously.
And the snake got them
before they got out

We felt the shock then
and feel the sting today.
And when the "compensation
for the loss" statements
come in ~~I feel sick~~

Dawn returns later that afternoon during my conference period. I am alive with enthusiasm.

"How you've improved this, Dawn! You're really pulling me into the experience."

"I couldn't believe how much longer it got."

"Not just longer, though, is it?"

"No, it's clearer."

"I really see your dad. It's like I can feel the sweat on my own face. I'll bet he didn't look anything like that when he went out."

"No, he was all dressed up. They both were. Mom wore a blue dress."

"That's quite a different image of them."

"They were really happy to be going out together after working that Saturday."

I shake my head at the irony. "The contrast increases the tragedy," I say. "You might include those details."

In the right-hand margin Dawn writes "blue dress."

"You know, Dawn, there was one word in here that hit me wrong."

"Which one?"

"Drinking."

"How come?"

"It might mislead readers."

"*Drinking* would?"

"Yeah. It makes me think of teenagers who go out drinking. But your parents didn't go out just to drink."

"No, they went out to be with their friends."

"That's what I mean. It was a night for dinner and friendship."

"I hadn't thought of *drinking* like that."

"Could just be me. Maybe I'm being picky—all your revision seems to have gone so smoothly."

"Not all smooth."

"No?"

"The ending doesn't seem right."

"Wonder why."

"I don't know. It's not complete."

"Maybe if you got particular again, this time about how the shock hit you, what you did."

"Maybe."

"You have something good in the ending, though."

" ' "Compensation for the loss" statements'?"

"Yes, and I'm glad you crossed out 'I feel sick.' "

"I know. It didn't work, but I need something."

"Well, you have the snake metaphor you created. You could work with that."

"How?"

"Extend it as you already have with *slithered, slid,* and *struck.* How can a snake make you sick?"

"I don't know what you mean."

I am struck by the feeling that I must go no further, that indeed I have already gone too far. "You think about it," I say. "I want to help you, but I don't want to make this my poem."

"OK."

"Let me ask you another question. That short third stanza that begins with 'They were happy.' Seems like there's more of a story behind it."

"There is."

"Are you going to go into it, give us some whys?"

"I don't know," says Dawn. Her voice is distant. "It's complicated. It's. . . ."

There is silence for a moment.

"You'll see whether you should or not," I say. "You have so much powerful stuff in this, Dawn."

"I'll work on it over the weekend," she says, "bring it in Monday."

In *The Art of Teaching Writing*, Lucy Calkins reminds readers that writing is an art (1986, 139). If all our conferences are merely content conferences that elicit information writers already know, then we are not giving the art its due. And we are not giving students opportunities to become artisans with written words.

In addition to content conferences, Calkins speaks of a number of other kinds. Design conferences, for example, deal with the shape or form of writing. A writer determines the structure of a particular piece of writing by interacting with the subject matter. *The Naked and the Dead, Catch-22*, and *Slaughterhouse-Five* all deal with World War II, but Mailer, Heller, and Vonnegut used vastly different structures for their novels. In design conferences we need to ask students questions that direct them to shape their visions, to make decisions about form.

In process and evaluation conferences, students reflect on the strategies they use to create writing and learn to look upon their creations with a critical eye. How do they write a draft? How do they work with a draft once it's written? What makes them realize that one point is irrelevant and another under-developed? When do they know they have an effective lead? Such conferences, writes Calkins, allow students to "teach us about themselves and their writing. These insights . . . provide the grounds for our teaching" (1986, 151).

Editing conferences occur during the final stage of the process, when correct copy is important for publication. Editing writing is comparable to what needs to be done to that beautifully beaten roll-top desk you found after searching a dozen second-hand antique shops. Once you've worked so hard finding that desk, it would be a shame not to polish the hardware, strip off the marred finish, sand the rough edges, and protect the surface with a lacquer that lets the natural wood grain show.

So conferences may address many different parts of the process of creating writing. Calkins presses us to remember that a writing conference rarely deals with only one of those parts. In truth, the parts blend in a wonderful tangle, just like the parts of the writing process.

When I asked Dawn about the four lines that began with "They were happy," my question dealt foremost with the content of the evolving poem. But her decision about whether to vivify those lines, leave them as they are, or delete them will affect more than the content. It will affect the poem's design, focus, dramatic movement, and impact.

During her revision, Dawn evaluated the final lines of her poem and felt they were incomplete. When I suggested she work more with her snake metaphor in order to solve the imbalance, she asked me a process question: "How?" If Dawn continues to extend the metaphor of the snake, the process of doing that will affect not only the quality of the poem, but also its content and design.

Monday morning Dawn walks into my room before school begins. Some of my homeroom students sit chatting in groups. Dawn's eyes are bright.

I greet her smile with my own. "How did it go?"
"Look."
She sets the poem in front of me.

(COMPENSATION)   (SNAKE)   (?)

Sweat poured off his face
as fleks of old black hay
clung to his bare chest and forearms
He stacked hay like a man getting older.
His wife sat atop the tractor
her black, greying hair in curlers
The click and whine of
the baler diminished all other sound
She pointed as she saw us
and they waved.

Mom pulled on her long pale blue dress
Dad straightened his tie.
as they went out to meet
their friends.
While they were talking and joking
the snake appeared in another
part of the club.

It slithered up and struck
When no one was looking
~~But is'nt that when~~
~~most bad things occur?~~

It slid through the halls
consuming chairs and tables
licking walls and carpet
with its tongue.
The snake's breathe touched
and smothered. . . .

No one took the bus boy seriously
And the snake had them

When my brother told us,
I did'nt cry much, until later,
just walked away and did'nt want to believe.
and when the "compensation
for the loss" statements
come in,
the venom is strong.

"Oh, Dawn—*venom*. The only word. I have to admit that
I was thinking of *poison* when I talked with you. But *venom*
is the word. You expanded the metaphor above there, too,
with the snake's tongue and breath."
She nods.
"What made you cross out those two lines?"
"They were on my mind a lot. I thought because I liked
them so much, but it was because they weren't right. It's
obvious."
"After your brother told you what happened, Dawn, where
did you walk away to?"
"The backyard."
"You want to put that in? That helps me place you."
She does.
"I feel a slight jump, kind of rushed in that second stanza
after 'their friends.'"
"Rushed?"
"Like I need a bridge between your parents going to meet
their friends and the snake striking. Let me give you the start

of a transitional line." I write in the margin, "And, later, amid . . ."

"Amid what?" asks Dawn.

"What must be going on around the people?"

"Music."

"Good. Anything else?"

"A lot of noise. Laughter, I'll bet."

"OK, think about it and see what you want to put in there."

"I'll put music and laughter."

We are quiet while she writes, and I decide to finally say something that's been on my mind since she brought in the second draft. "Instead of using 'his face' and 'his wife' in that first stanza, would it be better to use 'Dad's' and 'Mom'?"

There passes a silent moment of two heartbeats. "Yes," Dawn says, and writes those important words.

"I see you have a dilemma with the title."

"Yeah. Seems like I give something away if I use 'Compensation' or 'Snake.'"

"You're right. Those are more powerful as we discover them in the poem."

"But I don't know what I'll title it. I haven't been able to come up with anything else."

"Maybe I can, or you can ask some of your friends what they think."

"Anything. I'm tired of thinking about a title. What I have been thinking about is if the parts flow all right."

"The parts?"

"I have three different time periods: the day working in the field, that night, and afterwards."

"I didn't have any trouble with that. The skipped lines helped me."

"It still bothers me."

"You could use Roman numerals, if you like, or subtitles."

"No more titles!" she says. "Let's use Roman numerals."

We type Dawn's poem and publish it later that spring in the school's creative arts anthology.

THE LOSS

 I. Sweat poured off Dad's face
  as flecks of old black hay
  clung to his bare chest and forearms.
  He stacked hay like a man getting older.
  Mom sat atop the tractor,

her black, greying hair in curlers.
The click and whine of
the baler diminished all other sound.
She pointed as she saw us
and they waved.

II. Mom smoothed her long, pale blue dress.
Dad straightened his tie
as they left the house to meet
their friends.
And, later, amid music and laughter,
as they talked and joked,
the snake appeared in another
part of the nightclub.
It slid through the halls,
consuming chairs and tables,
licking walls and carpet
with its tongue.
The snake's breath touched
and smothered . . .

No one took seriously the busboy on stage.
And the snake had them.

III. When my brother told us,
I didn't cry much, until later,
just walked into the back yard,
didn't want to believe.
And when the
"compensation for the loss"
statements come in,
the venom is strong.

Dawn Koontz

"There is always the danger of appropriating the text and making it your own," writes Donald Murray, "forcing or manipulating the student into writing your vision in your language" (1985, 139).

I was guilty of that.

The closer Dawn's poem came to completion, the more directive I became in my comments and questions.

"You want to put that in?" I said. Translation: "Put that in."

I write in the margin, "And, later, amid . . ." Translation: "My words, my thinking are better than yours—in fact, since they are mine, let me do the actual writing. Step aside."

"OK, think about it and see what you want to put in there." Translation: "Only a fool would leave out these words. Surely you see how much more effective adding them would be."

I had been impressed by Dawn's powerfully revised poem. But as I read, I also made an agenda. And when I spoke with her, so intent was I to address each item I'd mentally listed that I completely ignored her utmost concern. Dawn's critical self-questioning about the three different time periods in the poem represents sophisticated thinking, involving content, design, evaluation, and editing. Very early during our final conference, I should have asked Dawn, "Is there anything I can help you with here?" or "Have you resolved all the problems that arose in working with this?"

Donald Graves points out that "listening to children is more a deliberate act than a natural one" (1983, 100). Listening to teenagers has become even less natural. After all, high-school English teachers have subject matter to transmit. We know *the* way to do things. We know how to construct a paragraph, how to excise redundancy, how to maintain a point of view, how to formulate a thesis. We know so much that students don't. We must fill them up with all we know. So we make dogma of minutia.

And in our haste to tell young writers how to do things, we forget that merely telling of new concepts doesn't usually lead to learning, and that students best learn what they're ready to learn, itching to learn. Dawn was concerned about the passage of time in her poem, had even intuitively skipped lines at appropriate places. Thankfully, she was enough at ease with me to bring up this problem after I'd finished with my own damnable agenda.

Dawn was ready to learn some of the ways that writers indicate abrupt time changes. The telling-teaching I did then, suggesting Roman numerals or subtitles as a way to make clearer the time shifts, undoubtedly had more impact upon her learning the art of writing than informing her of my perceived jump from one stanza to another or my perceived need for more information about what was going on in the night club.

Calkins urges us to invite writers "to claim their decision-making power" (1986, 146). We do this by helping them become their own readers. "The writing course," Murray points out, "is a writing and reading course" (1985, 139). Students growing as writers gradually raise their expectations for what they have written. They look at their words with an eye to improving them. Most of the things we say during our conferences should require students to consider closely their writing and take responsibility for its content, design, and creation.

Amid my exuberant ethical breaches, my tacit directives, I also asked Dawn questions that made her think and respond to the content, design, and creation of her poem. I have to work hard in conferences to keep my directives fewer than my questions. I want my students to understand that I expect them to be the masters of their writing, that I am not always going to come through with solutions to their problems, that indeed I don't always have solutions. And I try to keep in mind that any solution I might offer is merely a subjective one.

When I have conducted workshops on the topic of conferencing, some participants invariably complain that they cannot afford to take the time necessary to engage in writing conferences with every student. I must argue that writing teachers can ill afford *not* to take the time necessary to talk with students about their work. Too many positive things arise from teacher-student conferences. A writing class without them is severely limited.

In addition to internalizing conference procedures that teach them to interact with their words, students gain self-confidence and develop respect for writing when they engage in frequent conferences carried out in an atmosphere of acceptance and trust. Conferences tell students that their writing is so important the teacher will actually meet with them to discuss it and nothing else (Knapp 1976, 648). And because students have created the writing, have, in reality, put themselves on paper, when the teacher takes time to speak with them they understand that they, too, are significant. When students feel better about themselves, the writing teacher's job becomes easier.

But I concede that time is precious in a teacher's schedule. There is so much we want our students to experience and learn. Still, the value of conferences necessitates that we make room for them. On major pieces of writing, I usually need two or two and a half periods to meet with each writer in a classroom of twenty-five. That's about five minutes per student. Quick conferencing. The lengthier conferences I held with Dawn are a rarity.

Most of my conferences, in fact, are not like that. I talk with students in a variety of circumstances: quietly, while other class members are reading; quickly, during the last minutes of a period; and loudly, on occasion, when walking down the hall with a student amid change-of-class hubbub. A pointed question or a word of encouragement, regardless of the setting, can often be all that students need to find their way toward some strategy, some success.

The vast majority of my conferences though—maybe ninety-five percent of them, occur as I circulate about the classroom, while the students are engaged with their writing. Some students are at work on a specific part of their writing: drafting new leads, creating vivid, particular detail to replace general statements and vague descriptions, working pertinent dialog into a narrative, tightening wordy passages. Some are engaged in peer conferences in small groups or pairs. Some are generating new ideas through brainstorming or mapping exercises. Some are goofing off.

That last bit of truth comes with the territory of secondary-school instruction. Most students, I believe, we can reach and move to work productively in class. But a small percentage of students we cannot. For whatever reasons—personal, psychological, or social—they foil our best efforts. This might convince some teachers that it is impossible to conduct conferences with teenagers in class and still maintain a workshop atmosphere. This may be true for some teachers.

We know that a teacher's personality, strength of character, and commitment to student learning and growth directly affects the way students go about their work. A teacher unable to convince students that the purpose of the writing class is to work with writing probably fails to include conferencing as part of the class. That teacher probably also fails to cut students loose and get them to value their own voices, respect writing, play with words, exercise options, and question themselves about their drafts.

In discussing the importance of oral responses to students' writing, I have neglected the value of written response. I don't mean to. There are times when written responses are practical, helpful, even suddenly inspirational. When a paper has been completed, a final written response from the teacher can be pointed, appreciative, encouraging, and challenging. In writing, a teacher can often efficiently direct a writer's attention to a particular word or line. A single written word or phrase can swiftly indicate something well done.

I tout conferencing because it is so immediately human. A written response does not feature an open, helpful facial expression, eyes that show interest, a human voice repeating a writer's words and asking genuine questions based upon them. Further, the give-and-take of dialog allows us to avoid misunderstanding by clarifying our questions and listening to students' responses. We learn what they know and what they need to learn.

This chapter is chiefly about conferencing. But because I wrote of a specific case history of one teacher, one student, and one poem, the chapter had to be about other things as well: psychology (both a writer's and a teacher's), poetic inspiration, metaphorical thinking, revision, the power of precise imagery, and the transformation of experience, however tragic, into art, into a kind of triumph.

The chapter is also about the immense power, the great influence, of teachers. Some thrive on that power. Others who seek to make learners more independent are uneasy with the direct effect they often have on another person's life.

Children always remember their first teachers—father, mother, and siblings. We who have entered the teaching profession have assumed the position of directly influencing those beyond our immediate kinship. We speak a word of praise or a word of criticism, and someone we've known only weeks may be permanently changed in some way.

Teachers stay with us always. Lucy Calkins's *The Art of Teaching Writing* is full of references to her former teacher, Donald Murray. In turn, Donald Murray acknowledges his debt to Mortimer B. Howell of Tilton Junior College, his freshman English teacher. Like it or not, we teachers must live with our influential role. And more importantly, we must live up to it.

A former student of mine drops by and tells me that I influenced his decision to become a teacher. "I liked the way you taught us," he says. "I even started to like English. I thought I could reach kids in a woodworking class the same way you reached me." A teacher who attended a presentation of mine tells me I brought many things together for her and that it's influenced the way she's taught since then. Initially, I am flattered and delighted to hear such news, but then I think back to that class or presentation and hope that my model and my words were true, that what I said and did was from the heart.

And then, I stop short.

"Hold on," I say to myself. "You're being oversensitive and egotistical. It was more them than you. They were ready. Any number of teachers could have had the same effect on them at that point."

That's true, of course. The learner is all.

But, oh, what a difference we make with those learners who are ready, with those who become ready in our classes. We respond, we encourage, we nurture. We fan the embers so the potential flame may have a chance one day to blaze brightly, perhaps even roar and shoot straight to the heavens. We ask the questions that writers can answer, and gradually they learn to ask their own.

In Chapter 3, "Please Write," I included a poem in progress of my own that I had shown my students to illustrate that I, too, engaged in writing, that I, too, wrote imperfectly and unclearly, encountering and creating problems to surmount. After that conference with my students, I worked on the poem further, but remained unsatisfied and was unable to bring it to completion. Even so, I kept the poem on my desk.

A year and a half later, while taking a course with Donald Graves at the University of New Hampshire, I wrote those loosely joined lines of the poem in the learning journal we kept for his course. When he read them, Graves wrote in the margin, "Oh, I wish you'd share this next week in class."

His enthusiasm for the lines was all I needed to type the poem and work with it at intervals over the next week. I brought it to a point of completion, was happy with how I'd worked out the problem after all those months. That week I read the poem in class, then sent it to *Learning*, which rejected it, then to *English Journal*, which accepted it.

Of course, I have finished poems and other pieces of writing without the response of a sensitive, encouraging teacher. Would I have finished "Accountability" if Don Graves hadn't given me a genuine boost? I don't know. But when I was ready, I'm glad I was near a teacher who caused me to burn a little brighter, bright enough to see clearly into myself and find what I needed.

ACCOUNTABILITY

Let me push you over the cliff's edge.
You'll have to cooperate
By venturing near there.
When first you feel the pressure of my hand,
Don't dig in your heels and lean back.
You may cling to me,
But only lightly
So that when I give that final touch
(Or shove, if necessary),
Your fingers will rip cleanly free.
Just to be sure, I'll wear a tear-away sport coat.
You'll plummet through darkness,
Struggling to right your dangerous headfirst dive,
Wheeling your arms to gain new balance.
And just before you give up,
Just before the impact of failure,
You'll land,
Disoriented,
Bewildered,
Then happily astonished
To find
That you are
On your feet.

REFERENCES

Arbur, Rosemarie. 1977. "The Student–Teacher Conference." *College Composition and Communication* 28 (December):338–42.

Calkins, Lucy McCormick. 1983. *Lessons from a Child*. Portsmouth, NH: Heinemann.

————. 1986. *The Art of Teaching Writing*. Portsmouth, NH: Heinemann.

Ciardi, John. 1966. "One Writer's Work Habits." In *On Writing by Writers*, edited by William W. West. Boston: Ginn and Co.

Duke, Charles R. 1975. "The Student-Centered Conference and the Writing Process." *English Journal* 64 (December):44–47.

Elbow, Peter. 1973. *Writing Without Teachers*. New York: Oxford University Press.

Graves, Donald H. 1983. *Writing: Teachers & Children at Work*. Portsmouth, NH: Heinemann.

Graves, Donald, and Hansen, Jane. 1983. "The Author's Chair." *Language Arts* 60 (February):176–83.

Gutschow, Deanna M. 1975. "Stopping the March Through Georgia." In *On Righting Writing*, edited by Ouida H. Clapp. Urbana, IL: National Council of Teachers of English.

Hansen, Jane. 1983. "Authors Respond to Authors." *Language Arts* 60 (November–December):970–76.

Heller, Joseph. 1955. *Catch-22*. New York: Dell Publishing Co.

Knapp, John V. 1976. "Contract/Conference Evaluations of Freshman Composition." *College English* 37 (March):647–53.

Macrorie, Ken. 1984. *20 Teachers*. New York: Oxford University Press.

Mailer, Norman. 1948. *The Naked and the Dead*. New York: Holt, Rinehart and Winston.

Murray, Donald M. 1978. "Teaching the Motivating Force of Revision." *English Journal* 67 (October):56–60.

————. 1982. "The Listening Eye: Reflections on the Writing Conference." In *Learning by Teaching: Selected Articles on Writing and Teaching*. Upper Montclair, NJ: Boynton/Cook.

————. 1985. *A Writer Teaches Writing*. 2d ed., a complete revision. Boston: Houghton Mifflin Co.

Romano, Tom. 1986. "Accountability." *English Journal* 75 (March):90.

Vonnegut, Kurt. 1969. *Slaughterhouse-Five: or, The Children's Crusade*. New York: Dell.

————. 1976. *Slapstick: or, Lonesome No More!* Delacorte Press/Seymour Lawrence.

CHAPTER

Making the Grade in Evaluation:
Keep Students Writing

"What grade did I get?"
"I'll give you five dollars for every A on your report card."
"What do I need to pass?"
"I didn't give that kid an F; he earned it."
"This grade will kill my chance to go out this weekend."
". . . get into Honor Society."
". . . attend college."
". . . secure a good job."
". . . advance to GO."
". . . enter heaven."

Everybody, it seems, wants students to get grades—parents, guidance counselors, scholarship committees, college admission offices. Even employers, I am told, often want to know how students did in school—that is, what kind of grades they got. So I am required to evaluate students' work and translate those evaluations into letter grades. And I comply. I assign grades to individual pieces of writing; I assign final grades for courses.

I used to agonize about grading and spend heaps of time justifying grades. I don't any longer, which isn't to say I never ponder overlong about whether to assign a C+ or B−, an A− or B+.

The grades I assign these days, both for individual papers and a semester's work, are higher than the grades I dealt out in the early years of my teaching. Compared to science, math, and social-studies teachers, I am a pushover for grades. At six weeks' grading time I learn that over twenty percent of the sophomores have failed American Studies. For some reason the American Revolution is not their cup of tea. And they've been shown the consequences of failing to take and memorize extensive lecture notes. By contrast, no one has failed my sophomore writing class, except one student who is chronically absent, who is convinced that school does not want to hear what he thinks. Even when present, he refuses my invitations to write.

The grade distribution in my writing classes does not conform to the bell-shaped curve I learned about in Ed. Psych. 101. I rarely grade final pieces below a C −. Although my perception of grading is out of sync with my colleagues in math, science, and social studies, it is in harmony with the art teachers. That comforts me. Writing is creating. It is skill, craft, art. Practice, process, and passion are crucial to the development of quality product.

Higher grades weren't always the norm in my writing classes. When I began teaching and taught by my own version of the "Due Friday" process model, each graded set of papers contained two or three F's, five or six D's, and so on, climbing right over the top of the bell and swooping down the other side. My grading criteria were depth of content and strict adherence to conventional punctuation, standard usage, and correct spelling. The more errors a paper featured, the more I emphasized the criterion of strict adherence to rules of grammar and punctuation in determining a grade. I wasn't always aware I was doing that. Editing errors worked on me like Dr. Jekyll's potion, each sentence fragment turning me ever more heinous.

I wrote in red ink all over my students' papers. I marked them the way a delinquent might deface someone's personal property. And I was picky. One boy, I remember, looked incredulously at his low grade and the multitude of red writing I'd produced for him. He raised his hand and ingenuously asked, "Do you give the grade before or after you do the marking?"

I understood what he was getting at, all right. Naturally, I put the grade on *after* I had done the marking. How else was I to know just how bad the paper was? Most of the comments I wrote pointed out shortcomings in the students' writing. I did this, of course, in order to justify the low grades

I assigned. I had to convince students that they should feel lucky to get away with the grades they got. A rare line of positive commentary was lost in a paragraph of negative.

I've changed since those days. Working with teenagers through the processes of their writing has effected that change. Now I evaluate and assign grades to individual papers and a semester's work in relative serenity. The anguish and righteousness are gone. In my response I no longer am compelled to point out every language blunder of my students. In fact, when I put down a grade and respond to a student that final time for a particular paper, both my response and the grade are calculated to induce the student to write again. My students are most concerned about now. I am most concerned about their writing future.

TEACHER RESPONSES THAT AFFECTED MY WRITING FUTURE

In high-school English classes I received mostly B's, occasionally A's. My junior and senior years we wrote plenty, almost exclusively essay answers on tests and independent book reports, one each six weeks. To guide us in writing expositions about our books, the teacher gave us a detailed outline to follow. We began by writing a brief account of the author's life and then proceeded down the outline, discussing how a dozen standard literary terms related to the novel. I remember sitting in study hall, plodding through each part of the outline, sometimes fabricating in earnest when I hadn't a clue, for instance, how symbolism figured in *The Return of the Native*. For the most part, I did journeyman writing on those reports—except on one occasion.

That occurred when I read *Nineteen Eighty-Four*. Orwell's vision had stirred me so much that even the routine of the outline couldn't blunt my desire to write. The book contained a little bit of sex and a government that reminded me of the much-despised Nazi Germany. Both subjects were, and still are, of great interest to seventeen-year-old boys.

Contained in my report was my own version of Newspeak, that official language of Oceania meant to limit and control people's thinking. In addition to *printing* the Newspeak words amid my laborious handwriting, I was careful to ensure that context would enable the teacher to understand the words I made up. When I handed in my work, I felt good about both Orwell and my idea for writing the report.

The response I got, though, did not make me want to write again. The teacher directed me to refrain from making up new words. The English language, she pointed out, was composed of a rich enough lexicon for communication. And, with a peremptory exclamation point, she revealed to me that all through the report I had consistently misspelled *Nazi*. (This was the first hint that my visual memory for spelling was a poor one. But my ear was pretty good. I was so certain I'd heard a *t* in *Nazi* it never occurred to me to check its spelling.)

There was one other response to my writing I remember from high school. I'd given the same teacher an argumentative literary essay that I'd written on my own. At the time, pop radio stations were playing Simon and Garfunkel's "I Am a Rock." The song advocates an emotionally protected life in order to avoid psychic anguish. "A rock feels no pain," sang Paul and Art in the final lines of the song, "and an island never cries."

In my essay I passionately disputed the theme. I argued that pain and tears were worth risking for the chance to experience happiness and joy. "A rock might not feel pain," I wrote, "but it cannot love either." The teacher made no marks on the text of my paper but wrote in the top margin. "Tom, you sound just like one of those English poets!" Indeed I did, thought I. No John Keats, maybe, but a writer nonetheless.

In my college freshman English class I knocked about with B's and C's, trying to write well, but utterly confounded about how to compose an effective classification or definition paper. Upon their return to me, my essays were always messy with the instructor's markings, rhetorical questions, and at least one devastating, incisive comment that made me take the grade I'd received and run.

The sole exception to this cycle of writing and running was the final exam. I remember vividly the instructor's response to that. We'd been given a short poem to explicate. I interpreted the poet's words as a desperate plea to God to show himself, to give some sure sign of his existence. The poem articulated my vague religious anxieties. I connected personally with it and so caught fire in the balcony of that creaky lecture hall, where I sat packed with hundreds of other freshmen at Miami University in the spring of 1968.

I began writing in the standard mode of objective, lifeless exposition many of us had come to understand the university wanted. The topic was so strong in me, however, that I slipped naturally into my own desperate, almost angered plea to God. Certainly I wanted to do well in that class. English was my major. But most of my fire and boldness arose from recent personal experiences that had left me with religious doubt and confusion. If anyone needed comfort from a sure God, needed to be reassured that there was indeed purpose and logic to our living, I did. The essay fairly wrote itself.

A couple days later I went to see the instructor about my grade. He retrieved my blue book from the alphabetized pile on his desk. He began reading aloud his marginal commentary on my paper, which simply described what I was doing at that point in the text. He'd written a terse, running narrative of my writing. About halfway through, he read something like, "Romano breaks through the dry exposition! First-person Romano emerges! Voice—strong! Prose—crisp!"

My heart thumped to his words. Surely I had written well. And that should have been enough. But as an unconfident youth, I needed the teacher's appreciation of my words, his encouraging praise. I'd needed it a long time before that final paper. But even then it wasn't too late. I walked out of that office with summer ahead of me, confident I could write well again.

During my junior and senior years, I took four prose writing classes with Milton White. On my papers he wrote:

"You are getting better all the time, Romano."

"You may never sell it—it's too gentle. But my gosh, *I* like it. What a pleasure to watch you develop!"

"Romano! Romano! Bello, bello! I don't care what anyone else says, *me,* I loved it! Jeez, you've made progress. I'm so proud of you!!"

In rereading these comments from old papers I've kept all these years, I am surprised by Milton's exuberance. He'd have groaned in feigned agony had we used so many exclamation points in our stories. I was not one of the best writers in Milton's classes—not by a long shot. Junior year I got B's from him. Senior year I got A's in his writing seminar. I believe everybody did. And I was awed by most of my peers in that class, a group of excellent writers and critical readers.

But Milton wasn't interested in comparing students. He was interested in good writing and in helping his students produce it. So he kept us riding high, optimistic and eager. We wanted to write again when we got our papers back. Of course, swift words of praise were not all Milton gave us. Both in our papers and during class discussion, he taught us specific points of style, language, and taste. But mainly, Milton kept us aloft.

GRADING INDIVIDUAL PAPERS

Students write many things I do not grade: exploratory writing, brainstorming, freewriting, experimental play with words, responses to films or readings, journal entries, drafts. Early in a semester a student will invariably ask, "What grade did I get on this?" I tell him the truth: "I can't possibly grade or comment on all the writing you need to do if I expect you to become a better writer. You need to write a lot. Trying to grade it all would drive me mad. And anyway, I want to grade you at your best, so I'll grade only pieces that you've carried through to publication."

Depending on the class, this could be from four to eight pieces a semester.

The actual grading of a piece of writing represents only a small portion of the time I spend teaching young writers. I've read most of their nongraded writings. I've often read and responded informally to their journals. And I've conferenced with them about various drafts they've written in bringing pieces to publication. I am heavily into their vision and progress.

Certainly, the most significant learning of the craft of writing occurs when students are generating their own language and interacting with it. Our grades and written comments don't teach nearly as much as we think. Still, the grades we give and the comments we make—our final responses to particular pieces of writing—often have far-reaching effects on students' attitudes toward writing, on their willingness to write in the future. And, thus, evaluation and grading of papers become crucial in a traditional school setting where, more than anything else, teachers want students to *practice* the craft of writing.

When I hand papers back, students quickly check the grade, then read the response I've written. Although the grade is of most immediate interest to them, my personal words about their words are a key to their continued growth. Above all, I want the tone of my response to communicate my respect for the students' words and visions, for their willingness to put both on paper.

I want the writers I teach to feel good about their writing, to want to write again. That is no mean feat. I know, because occasionally I leave my writing not wanting to write again. Sometimes I am frustrated and overwhelmed by the hard work of getting words the way I want them. If I find writing difficult, I who love to write, I know many of my students do. And I want to be there for them, supportive of their efforts, appreciative of their work.

Much may go amiss in writing before something goes right. I continue to be duped by my own written words. I think they're doing one thing when they're doing something else. I believe they're doing this when they aren't doing this at all. I work hard trying to be clear, logical, and effective. So when I err, I don't need someone pummeling me with it. What I need is someone encouraging me, pointing out often what I'm doing right and well, and gently helping me see weaknesses in my writing—like Milton did.

In grading and evaluating papers I reward students for working hard in the process of writing, for participating in good faith. If students try techniques we've talked about, I reflect my appreciation of that in my evaluation. The grade I assign also gives students a feel for the quality of a particular piece of writing, though I don't have to be concerned much with this. In a class in which everyone's work is shared, students soon begin to recognize quality writing. And, inevitably, they make judgments about their own performance, talents, and progress.

Evaluation of writing is a necessarily subjective act. Objectivity is impossible. Participate in one group grading session and you'll realize that. When many teachers evaluate the same paper, their judgments of its merit are diverse and astounding. So I am left with my subjectivity. When I evaluate papers, I bring to bear my history as a writer, my tastes in reading, my prejudices and moods, my ever-developing understanding of teenagers, and my perceptions of how a particular student will be affected by what I say. Yes, *who* the student is helps determine what grade I give, what response I make. It cannot be otherwise. Each of my students is an individual. A paper of similar quality may be a C for Mary, an A for Max.

I have no foolproof grading system. I don't grade 50% for content and 50% for mechanics. I don't make the final grade contingent upon one more rewrite. I have no checklist beside me as I read student papers, awarding or subtracting points in various rhetorical categories. I'm willing to let the writing do what it intends to do. Do not believe, however, that I am looking for nothing when I read and evaluate student writing.

I am looking for writing that works, the same thing I anticipate when I open a novel, take a first plunge into a poem, or begin an editorial. When I read my students' final drafts, I hope to be knocked out, floored, bowled over, and generally wowed.

I'm looking for information that makes me crave more information, gives it to me, and then makes a point.

I'm looking for surprises of language and vision.

I'm looking for vivid images.

I'm looking for rhythms of language and voice.

I'm looking for an adept employment of some naturally evolved form that might even prompt me to utter aloud my appreciation as I sit alone reading.

It's happened. I usually get a good deal of what I'm looking for. The students have worked hard developing it all through their writing processes. And, I should add, part of their success can be attributed to my success, for I've been working hard at my teaching processes.

I start grading a set of papers, say twenty-five, by reading through them. No pen do I hold, ready to dive amid the students' words. I simply read to be moved by the writing. During this step, I make preliminary judgments of quality. As I finish the pieces, I place them in piles, according to my perceptions of their effectiveness. I'm trying to assess honestly how well each piece of writing works. When I finish reading a set of papers, I have four, five, six, sometimes seven piles.

I clip together all the papers in each pile and then arrange the piles from the most effective to the least effective. Next, I try to let some time pass, sometimes hours, sometimes a couple of days. Then I start with the pile I thought was best, reread each paper, maybe browse back through the pages, looking again at those passages or pages that worked. I consider the student, what he's attempted, what language skills he's improved, and finally assign a grade. The papers in that first pile will usually be in the A range, although I always discover I've overestimated one or two. Later on, I will discover that I've underestimated the quality of other papers or not considered the particular student enough. This method of grading keeps me aware of what kind of quality my students are producing and also enables me to address each individual's needs.

I don't mark these final papers. I don't write anything on them. Not a word. Not one cryptic squiggle. I don't even write the grade on the paper. Their neatly prepared copy is returned to them in the same condition it was given to me— with one exception. On their copy I clip or staple my response, usually typed since I now have a computer to do word processing.

Here is my response to the first piece of writing that Dwayne carried through to publication not quite one month into the first semester of his sophomore year:

> Your revision paid off, Dwayne. The arguments are much clearer and stronger. Congratulations. I especially like your reasons for telling the reader that he won't need much top-end power. The great low-end power will already have him ahead of everybody!
> spelling   B –

Here's the piece that prompted my response and grade (Figure 8–1 shows the piece in Dwayne's own handwriting):

KAL OR BUST

Well this is for all you Honda Riders. Before you say Honda is the best, ride a Kawasaki (KX). Kawasaki Has the best suspension, called Uni Track.

When you ride a Kawasaki it is easy to go threw ruts and groves, just like flowing Water. They dont Bounce around and make it hard to control.

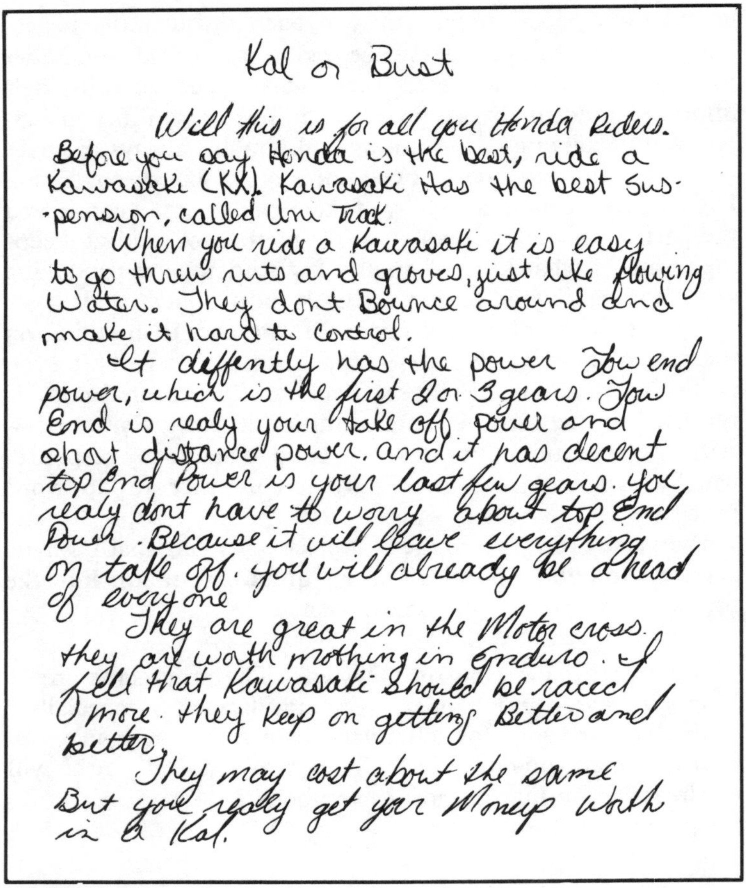

> ### Kal or Bust
>
> Will this is for all you Honda Riders. Before you say Honda is the best, ride a Kawasaki (KX). Kawasaki Has the best sus-pension, called Um Track.
>
> When you ride a Kawasaki it is easy to go threw ruts and groves, just like flowing Water. They dont Bounce around and make it hard to control.
>
> It diffently has the power Low end power, which is the first 2 or 3 gears. Low End is realy your take off power and short distance power. and it has decent top End Power is your last few gears. You realy dont have to worry about top End Power. Because it will leave everything on take off. you will already be a head of every one
>
> They are great in the Motor cross. they are worth mothing in Enduro. I fell that Kawasaki should be raced more. they keep on getting Better and better.
>
> They may cost about the same But you realy get your Money worth in a Kal.

FIGURE 8–1

It diffintly has the power Low end power, which is the first 2 or 3 gears. Low End is realy your take off power and short distance power. and it has decent top End Power in your last few gears. You realy dont have to worry about top End Power. Because it will leave everything on take off. you will already be a head of every one.

They are great in the Motor cross. They are worth nothing in Enduro. I fell that Kawasaki should be raced more. they keep on getting Better and better.

They may cost about the same But you realy get your
Moneys Worth in a Kal.

Dwayne Chrisman

The writing of high-school students cannot be evaluated
out of context. I consider what they have gone through in
creating the piece, what they have tried that they've never
tried before, what they have written in the past, and what
they may write in the future. Although Dwayne broke many
rules of writing convention in this piece, he also did many
things right, things that we had talked about and worked on
in class.

His voice is strong and authentic. He has chosen to write
about what he knows. And he carried this piece through four
drafts, which surprised me, considering Dwayne's professed
antipathy toward writing. During the revisions, he expanded
and clarified his points from an earlier draft. "They deffently
have the Power. Low End Power." became "It diffintly has
the power Low end power, which is the first 2 or 3 gears.
Low End is realy your take off power and short distance
power."

While sharing a draft of the piece with a small group of
his peers, Dwayne also came to realize that he should alter
his tone to fit the audience (the other motorcycle riders in
class). Since he was trying to convince the other boys to ride
a Kawasaki, Dwayne decided to cut this disdainful, abrasive
sentence from his first draft: "But if you are a wimp and can't
ride get a Honda or something."

So Dwayne is doing much right. And a B− seemed appropriate for him and his accomplishment on this paper. On
future pieces we will attend to some of his errors in writing
etiquette. Spelling is one of them, which I noted discreetly
at the bottom of my written response. When it comes time
for Dwayne to edit his next piece, I'll ask him to take special
care with spelling. In fact, he will have written on the inside
cover of his writing folder that spelling is one of his editing
problems. But right now and always, I want to remind him
of what he's doing right, of work well done.

I want to show him I value and reward good-faith
participation.

I want to keep him encouraged.

I want him to write again.

In the next weeks we worked hard at packing our writing with vivid, significant detail—showing, not telling. I used an idea from Rebekah Caplan (1981) of the Bay Area Writing Project. I gave the students a "telling" sentence like, "The dog was mean" or "The child was incredibly filthy." From there the students wrote a paragraph or two *showing* what the sentence told. I randomly picked five of the writings, read each aloud anonymously, and let the class grade them—A, B, or C, the sole criterion being how well the writing showed things, rather than told them. After grading, I disclosed the author's name.

For the next piece to carry through to publication, Dwayne chose to write about his pit-bull puppy. He often spoke of his pup, and he had recently been reading about pit bulls. Dwayne was loaded with information from both books and personal experience. I figured he'd be into this topic even more than motorcycles. I conferenced with Dwayne twice— once during his planning, and once after I'd read his first draft.

In the last conference he had located spots in the text where readers might not visualize scenes, where I, a reader, hadn't. Dwayne marked his draft with marginal notes. He also wrote numbers within the text. His plan was to write additional sentences on a separate sheet of paper. The new passages would be coded by corresponding numbers to those in the text. This would help Dwayne remember where to insert his newly created writing when he made a fresh copy.

But when I read the final version of "My Pup," I was disappointed as a reader and confounded as a teacher. Dwayne hadn't carried out his plans. He hadn't really tried to capture his pup with vivid, particular detail, the kind we had worked so hard to incorporate into our writing, the kind he appeared to be heading toward during our last conference.

I gave his paper a C – and wrote this response:

> I think my favorite things about this, Dwayne, are the
> first and last sentences. The first gets right to the subject
> matter and the last contains humor and makes for a
> good ending. You know so much about dogs that I
> would really have liked to see you *show* me more. I'd
> like to have heard, seen, and felt your pup. What's his

name, anyway? I'd like to have heard your commands to him and seen him respond.

Spelling and paragraphing are the editing skills you must work on. Count the number of paragraphs you have in this piece.

Three months later, in looking through Dwayne's writing folder, I read everything he'd written on his way to "My Pup." I found second and third drafts of the piece. In six different spots Dwayne had written vividly detailed passages about his pup, creating some of the very images I'd found missing. One rapidly written, unpolished, unedited addition read "he look Bad when he walk if you know how a Pit Bull walks the legs look stiff But they aren't there just so muscular they just kind of strut along."

Why hadn't Dwayne included these revisions in his final copy? I asked him and discovered a strategy of mine that had temporarily backfired.

"The day I was gonna make the final copy I got to class late," said Dwayne. "I didn't have a lot of time, and I didn't like reading the first piece up on the author's stool in front of the class. So I thought I'd just make the pup story shorter by copying the first draft without the changes I made."

We looked through his folder together, and I noted that on his next two published pieces he hadn't been governed by the "shorter is better because I won't be reading it long" philosophy.

"I figured since I was gonna hafta read my writing to the class anyway," said Dwayne, "it wouldn't hurt to be reading a little longer. Plus, I like it when the class gets a kick outa what I write."

Fifteen days after "My Pup," three months into the semester, my sophomores brought their next piece, a character sketch, to the publication stage. Here is Dwayne's (Figure 8–2 shows the piece in Dwayne's own handwriting):

CHARLIE MY COUSIN

Charlie is a seven year old boy in the first grade for the second time. He is always getting into trouble.

In school one day, he was setting in class chewing tab-

FIGURE 8–2

CHARLIE MY COUSIN

Charlie is a seven year old boy in the first grade for the second time. He is always getting into trouble.

In school one day, he was setting in class chewing tabbacco. He had his jaket on and a cup inside it for his spit. He made it to obvious and he got caught. Instead of going to the teacher, like a good little boy would do. He ran! and hide. The teacher had the ~~prince~~ principal looking for him. He found Charlie in a empty class room under a desk just a chewing away. The principle just warned him not to do it again.

About two or three weeks later, he was in the gym and had to go to the restroom. Instead of going to the teacher and asking to go to the restroom. He took the lazy way out and went under the bleachers. This time he didn't get a warning. He got a paddling.

When he walks, he looks like a rooster, his arms out, his head back. Most of his pants are to big. When he walks he kinda jumps and pulls them up.

He is constantly aggravating other kids, interrupting a game or calling them names just to get them to chase him. When he gets into a argument he always has to have the last word in.

He is always flinging his stringy blonde hair out of his eyes and smiling with his two big teeth in front that are a cream color. The rest are either rotten or caped.

When he is out of tabbacco, he walks up to my house and says Grandpa "Give me a chew" He does But it is to strong. Charlies eyes get big like it is burning him up. He looks like he is ready to puke. But he won't spit it out. He says "He loves the taste". But his favorite is Red Ox.

The End

baco. He had his jaket on and a cup in side it for his
spit. He made it to obvious and he got caught. Instead
of going to the teacher, like a good little boy would do.
He ran! and hide. The teacher had the principal looking
for him. He found Charlie in a empty class room under
a desk just a chewing away. The principle just warned
him not to do it again.

About two or three weeks later. He was in the gym
and had to go to the restroom. Instead of going to the
teacher and asking to go to the restroom. He took the
lazy way out and went under the bleachers. This time
he didn't get a uarning. He got a paddling.

When he ualks, he looks like a rooster, his arms out,
his head back. Most of his pants are to big. When he
walks he kinda jumps and pulls them up. He is constantly aggravating other kids, interupting a game or
calling them manes just to get them to chase him. When
he gets into a argument he always has to have the last
word in.

He is always flinging his stringy blonde hair out of his
eyes and smiling with his two big teeth in front that are
a cream color. The rest are either rotten or caped.

When he is out of tabbaco, he walks up to my house
and says Grandpa "Give me a chew" He does. But it is
to strong. Charlie's eyes get big like it is burning him
up. he looks like he is ready to puke. But he won't spit
it out. He says "He loves the taste." But his favorite is
Red Ox.

The End

My response:

Dwayne, you have captured a delightful, ornery, active little imp. So many details bring him to life: "He
found Charlie in an empty classroom under a desk just
chewing away." Vivid. I also like how you varied the
sentence lengths in this piece. You follow a long sentence with a short one. That's effective. And the lead is
a grabber. You're really coming along as a writer. In
fact, you're coming along so well that you really must
put your mind to mastering the things I've listed below.
You should fool around with this piece some more, then

correct it so nothing's wrong, and then submit it to me
and I'll put it among the manuscripts to be considered
for *Menagerie*, the creative-arts anthology.
spelling and sentence sense   A –

In rereading my response, I spot one place where I definitely
had deluded myself: Charlie was not "delightful." But Dwayne's
progress was. One day I'd taught the class a minilesson on
leads, discussing their importance and showing the students
a variety of ways that professionals began pieces. We all went
to work then and wrote four or five leads for our pieces.
Dwayne's lead, "Charlie is a seven year old boy in the first
grade for the second time," shows he'd assimilated the concept
of lead writing.

I was also excited that Dwayne had varied his sentence
length, a technique we hadn't talked about in class. I'd told
the students that the main criterion for evaluating their sketches
would be how much life they could breathe into their characters
with words. This time Dwayne had provided the specific
information, the pertinent detail that made his writing work.
Tobacco-chewing Charlie leapt from the page.

I look at the A – I gave Dwayne on this piece and wonder
if the grade was too high. Maybe. I wanted him to do well
after the C – on the previous paper. Perhaps I went overboard.
Look at all Dwayne's errors of usage, style, spelling, and
punctuation! Shouldn't these have substantially affected his
grade? No, I decided. Dwayne had gained too much on this
piece. I wasn't going to obliterate that by grading him down
because of his struggle with writing conventions.

I remind myself that although a few sentences stand as
unintentional fragments, he wrote thirty complete sentences.
I also note that he'd done some self-diagnosis of his spelling
problems. On a draft he had circled *constintly* and *agervating*
and printed their correct spellings in the margin for later
recopying. In addition, Dwayne had shown me he practices
the process of writing, understands it is renovative. He has
the idea of dismantling and rearranging old material as well
as creating new material on his way to a final product. Dwayne
also showed signs of behaving as a craftsman, employing sentence rhythms effectively, using dialog, choosing vivid detail,
and ending some paragraphs with clinching final lines. There

is so much he's doing well. I am certain that Dwayne is feeling good about his writing and will write again.

I'll stand by the A −. On this paper. At this point in the semester. For Dwayne.

As a semester progresses, I raise my standards for quality. I explain to students that a B paper the third week of the semester might be a C paper the final week. This is no Catch-22. Far from it. I increase my expectations because I respectfully recognize my students' capacity for learning and growth. I tell them this plainly. I expect them to become more skilled at creating writing.

And they do. When teenagers work through writing processes, their final written products generally improve. The more experience they get in a safe writing workshop—practicing, experimenting, sharing, conferencing, getting timely instruction, connecting reading and writing—the more adept they become at producing quality writing of their own. It's inevitable. And its imperative for continued growth.

At the 1985 NCTE convention in Philadelphia, Lucy Calkins reminded her audience of the need for students to produce good work. "We process people don't often talk about the quality of written products," she said. "We talk drafts and revision, expression and discovery, and nudging and awareness, but we don't often talk about the need for excellence. And I think that's a mistake. Human beings have a primal need to do good work. If our children are going to care about writing, they need to see their writing getting better and better."

For Dwayne's final piece of graded writing first semester, he wrote a narrative about himself and two friends riding motorcycles one afternoon on some rough trails they had blazed. The story was almost twice as long as the character sketch. I wrote this in response:

> An action-based story, Dwayne. It moves. And I like your description of the blackness after the crash and how different things looked like snapshots. The cat-and-mouse game you and Jerry played with the lead—good! I commend you on your title and subtitle: "Crash and Burn: A Rapid Day Down by the River." Not every story should be subtitled. But some should, like this one. Your reading has influenced your writing. If you

keep trying ideas that professional writers use, you may
be a pro yourself someday, writing about motorcycles.

On the editing side of things, you're improving. Have
cut down the spelling errors and sentence fragments.
Still, when you proofread you need to be tougher on
yourself and more doubting. You write too well to let
editing errors get in your reader's way.

Oh yeah! I also noticed that you used the word *lying*
correctly. Not many students do. How did you learn
that?

It's been good working with you this semester,
Dwayne. You grew quite a bit.

B

This is how I evaluate students' individual pieces of writing.
My method cannot be objective. I am human and doomed to
subjectivity. So I've tried to learn as much as I can about the
processes of creating writing and teaching writing. I want my
subjective self to be well grounded in the craft I teach.

I've heard of other methods for evaluating student writing,
ones that attempt to establish absolutely objective criteria and
thus deliver writing teachers from the throes of evaluation
and grading:

. . . A college professor wouldn't give students anything
above a B+ on papers. An A paper, he contended, indicated
excellence. To be excellent a piece of writing had to be published
in *The New Yorker*. None of his students had ever done that;
therefore. . . .

. . . In its crusade to eradicate sentence fragments, comma
splices, run-on sentences, and certain misspellings, a high-
school English department instituted an "automatic F" policy.
Teachers gave student papers two grades: one for content,
one for mechanics. If students committed any error that appeared on the department's "Auto F" hit list (which every
student was given a copy of), they received an F for mechanics.
Automaniacally. . . .

. . . My ninth-grade niece showed me a paper she'd written
about a horrible losing streak suffered by the Cleveland Browns.
She'd received a C+, an 82%. I marveled at the pinpoint
precision of the grade. There was no comment written on the
paper, no response attached. The teacher had marked four

comma splices, underlined and labeled two sentence fragments, and circled three misspelled words. At that point the pure science of mathematics took over the task of evaluation and grading. Each error equaled two percentage points. Nine errors times two. Subtract from perfection, 100% (a *New Yorker* piece, no doubt, one with fifty opportunities to commit error). Voila! 82%. No argument there. Grading couldn't be simpler.

In one part my niece had written:

> When asked about the Browns' record, quarterback Brian Sipe said, "I don't know. There's just something wrong with the Browns." Something wrong indeed.

Those last three words, indicative of voice and style and demonstrating a wry sense of irony, had been dutifully marked as a sentence fragment.

Apply purely scientific or mathematical systems to the evaluation of writing and you're asking for trouble. Human beings have a way of fouling inflexible systems, intentionally and unintentionally. The human heart and mind resist statistical analysis. So I have no foolproof, objective method for evaluating and grading a student's written words.

Furthermore, my method cannot divorce the writer from the writing. I've read articles in which authors stressed that when they evaluate student papers, they make clear that it is the writing being evaluated, not the student. Thus, they argue, even when evaluations are highly critical, the student maintains a positive self-image.

I don't believe it. Distinguishing between the student and the writing is a fool's distinction. Writing is the writer. It embodies her voice, her passion, her thinking, her intellect, her labor, and, on some occasions, her very soul.

"You are a fine person, but this piece of writing is a D." Don't kid yourself—when that happens, the writer is stung.

Such a method is directly opposed to our purposes as teachers. Our responses and grades should nurture. This does not mean we deceive students about their writing skills, offering overexuberance and undeserved praise. On the contrary, we owe them honesty. We must humanely discuss their writing problems and help them work to master them. But let us not forget that honesty also means we must continually strive to see what our students are doing well, and then acknowledge and reward it. What really matters is that our students keep writing, learning, and growing as much as they can.

At semester's end, I asked Dwayne and his fellow sophomores to write briefly about their own writing—how they felt about it, how their attitude had changed or stayed the same, what they'd learned. In part, Dwayne wrote:

> Last August I came in here dreading writing I always hated writing, but these last few months I've changed. The Beginning of a storie is my worst phase. But it is worth it at the end to see a B or a A— on my paper. I've learned that its more than a one time writing in a story you have to reread, revision, check spelling etc. in order for it to be good. I use to not be able to get what I'm thinking down on paper but I'm a little better, sometimes I get such a flow to write.

So at the end of a semester, Dwayne has a folder full of his own words. Some of them he's labored over, rereading, revising, checking spelling, and so forth. He has his conscious perceptions of what he's learned. He has his unconscious perceptions, too. As Dwayne explained to me, "Some stuff in your mind you don't know you got until the right time comes." He has my written responses to four of his papers. He has whatever he's remembered from conferences and other moments when he shared a final piece of writing or listened to someone else's. He has more writing experience. And he has a final grade, which I give him for his semester's work.

GRADING A SEMESTER'S WORK

We learn best, I think, through doing, through participating in good faith. To continue to learn gardening, for example, I garden. I till soil. I fertilize, plant, weed, cultivate, tend, harvest, and taste. I spend much time on my hands and knees, sweating in the garden, participating in good faith. I also talk to friends, read books and journals, and watch television programs about gardening. But always I go back to the garden and keep trying the things I'm learning and learning the things I'm trying.

At times I have failed miserably. Onions and potatoes have rotted in the wet ground because of my impetuosity to get them planted too early in spring. One year my ignorance of silk beetles ruined a small crop of sweet corn. Another year cutworms chewed through the stems of most of my young pepper plants, lopping them off at soil level. The first time I grew luffa gourds, I provided a ridiculously small wooden frame for the vines to climb. They swarmed over it, then wound their way into my asparagus and tomato plants, pulling down some of them.

Other times I have succeeded impressively. I have raised corn loaded with kernels nearly bursting with liquid sweet. I've picked broccoli florets in October so tender and deep green that fresh broccoli at the supermarket will forever be second-rate. I have grown fat Italian plum tomatoes and fragrant basil, combined them with butter, and created an aromatic pasta sauce that would have made my Grandmother Romano smile and nod her head in approval.

Because I keep sweating in the garden, learning by participating in good faith, both the failures and successes have been instructive.

To grow as writers our students, too, must participate in good faith, must do their own sort of sweating in the garden. They must write and interact with that writing. They must also read quality professional writing, share the work of their peers, talk about their writing processes and choices, and receive the response and timely instruction of a good teacher. All that will help. But the primary requirement for growth is frequent practice in the craft they are learning.

The amount of writing students do should be far more than a teacher can evaluate. Although I assign a letter grade only to those pieces that have been carried through the process, I note in my grade book all the instances when students have written—their journal entries, freewriting, exploratory writing, written responses to reading, drafts, even their just-plain fooling around with words.

If students turn in drafts on time, I place a check by their name in an appropriate column in the grade book. If we spend a day drafting leads, I write "Leads" in a column of the grade book and check the appropriate boxes for those students who participated, who put in their work with language on paper. By the time a semester is completed I might have 25 to 35 checkmarks in my grade book that indicate a student's good-faith participation. If the assignment or writing has been done particularly well or the student appears to have learned something from it, I indicate that in the grade book with a star or plus mark, something to remind me of the quality of the work the student has produced in good faith.

After reading an *English Journal* article by Sharilyn Calliou (1982), I devised my own way of deriving grades from these checkmarks and stars. If a student completes all the good-faith assignments, he receives a B. If he's completed some of them exceptionally well, I try to be reasonable and fair, raising the grade to reward the degree of merit. Some students will end up with A+'s. If a student has gaps in the grade book, indicating that participation has been something less than good faith, I lower the grade.

This grade for good-faith participation accounts for about half a student's semester grade. Thus, it isn't always the gifted students who achieve the highest grades in my classes. One of the best high-school writers I've worked with pulled a C+ one semester. He was a talented writer, still is (based upon the letters we occasionally exchange). Had he participated in good faith, I believe he would have grown and learned things neither I nor he could have imagined. I should also add that he was forthright, not given to self-deception, and, therefore, the C+ was no affront to him.

Evaluation and grading. They are the aspects of teaching writing we enjoy least. I'd much rather confer with a writer about her work in progress, listen in on a peer response group, help a student toward self-editing, or share final drafts. But periodically we must evaluate the work and progress of the teenagers we work with. When we do, we must always keep in mind that our responses and our grades help create their self-images as learners, help shape their attitude toward future writing. And in the future, above anything else, we want them to write again.

REFERENCES

Calkins, Lucy McCormick. 1985. Address at the 1985 National Council of Teachers of English Fall Convention, Philadelphia, PA.

Calliou, Sharilyn. 1982. "An Evaluation System Which Promotes Student Writing." *English Journal* 71 (March):90–91.

Caplan, Rebekah. 1981. Presentation at the Ohio Writing Project summer institute, June 22, 1981, Miami University, Oxford, OH.

Hardy, Thomas. 1928. *The Return of the Native*. New York: The Macmillan Co. (Originally published in 1878.)

Orwell, George. 1949. *Nineteen Eighty-Four*. New York: Harcourt, Brace and Co.

Simon, Paul, and Garfunkel, Art. "I Am a Rock." In *Sounds of Silence*. Columbia Records, 1965.

Writing Amid Literature
Part One: Other Than Essays

The possibilities excite the soul. Authors have written poetry of wide variety, plays about every social class, nonfiction of all sorts, fiction of countless styles, and other pieces that fit no single genre. All these forms are available for students to try in a literature class. And subject matter? If modern literature has taught us one thing, it is that any idea, experience, or emotion is a possible writing topic.

As English teachers our major responsibility is to enfranchise students in our classes to such a degree that they think of themselves as writers, as those who use written language to both discover thinking and communicate thought, who boldly try varied forms of writing, using them to meet their needs.

Traditionally, when most people thought about writing done in literature classes, they thought of essays. Students wrote expository papers and examinations on the literature they read. These are legitimate kinds of writing for literature classes, but in too many cases the essay—particularly the essay test answer—dominates the literature-based writing done by teenagers. Such repeated, narrow engagement in composition, I believe, prevents students from developing open, flexible attitudes about writing. It inhibits their ability to use writing as a learning tool, and it promotes habits of mind and perceptions of how writing is done that may cripple their growth as writers.

Make no mistake. My students write their share of thoughtful essays on literature, and I will discuss that genre at length in the following chapter. But over the years I have opened up my literature classes to include far more than essays. My students write to make their own literary artifacts, and they also use writing to connect personally with universal themes and subjects, to reveal their first impressions, and to uncover and sharpen their reading-thinking processes.

TO MAKE LITERARY ARTIFACTS

My American literature students were not digging Carl Sandburg's alliterative, onomatopoeia-packed, musical mood poem "Jazz Fantasia." We'd read other Sandburg poems, and the students had exhibited no such obstinate resistance. Finally, a reluctant but succinct voice clarified the problem.

"It's the jazz, man. Nobody listens to jazz."

"But don't you see?" I said. "You had to have jazz to have rock 'n' roll."

"Why?" came a belligerent voice from the back of the room.

I stepped forward a pace. "Because the music you like today didn't just spring from nowhere," I said. "There's a long history of good music in America, of musicians, all kinds, making their visions known in note and word. The rock today grew out of yesterday's jazz."

"Mr. Romano," said a girl whose eye makeup perfectly matched the color of her sweater, "I can't believe this jazz poem has anything to do with the music that's popular with me and my friends."

"In the early part of this century jazz *was* pop," I explained. "Jazz was hip, with-it. Why, if you had lived then, you probably would have been a jazz lover."

"No way!" shouted too many voices to count.

Though overwhelmed by superior numbers and youthful narrow-mindedness, I was still determined to make my point. Holden Caulfield had me pegged, too, when he said of Old Spencer in *The Catcher in the Rye*: "You can't stop a teacher when they want to do something. They just *do* it" (11).

"Sandburg was simply writing about the music of his time," I persisted. "Why, if he were a young poet today, he wouldn't have written 'Jazz Fantasia.' He would have written 'Rock Fantasia.'"

Everybody in the room, most of all me, was surprised by

what I'd said. And even the most hard-core teenage rocker, slouched in his seat, arms crossed in front of his favorite faded concert T-shirt knew I'd hit upon something: the linguistic-cognitive surprise, or "kaboom" as third grader Melissa had dubbed it. My desperate efforts at persuasion, at conjuring language that would convince those kids of my rightness had led me instead to a new idea, an eminently suitable writing assignment. My students would do with rock 'n' roll what Sandburg had done with jazz: in a free-verse poem they would capture the moods and sounds of their music with vivid imagery, colorful, alliterative language, and a funny, slangy enjoinder like Sandburg's "Go to it, O Jazzmen."

We went to work on "Jazz Fantasia." Never had my students studied a poem so closely to discover how a poet had crafted word and image to achieve effect. We talked about all the poetic devices, all the language play Sandburg had used to make words depict music. Then we talked about the writing assignment. Not all students, I discovered, liked rock 'n' roll, so we listed other kinds of music and their subcategories. Some students wrote "Country Fantasia," "Soul Fantasia," and "Gospel Fantasia." A few days later, when I collected their poems, so delightful were they that I read them aloud to the class, honoring the authors by giving each poem an animated oral interpretation. Here's one:

ROCK FANTASIA

Clink on your keyboard,
sing on your saxophone,
drop on the hard beating drums.
Get with it, you Rock Master.

Swing your fingers on the strings
of the loud electric metal,
make your drums crash and
sting the ears with the piercing keys.

Soothe like a refreshing drink
on a dry afternoon,
soothe like a killer back rub,
jump like lightning diving in the sky.

You Rock Master, single out the
lonely guitar—make people scream
as if they just saw a ghost and
paralyze them with fear.

Break the set . . . now a bird sings
softly in the old oak tree with a
high chirp . . . and the light
feathers ruffle in the air . . . a cool
breeze runs through the restless
trees . . . get with it, you Rock Master!

Sybil McGee, junior

With the writing of this assignment my students climbed
a pinnacle in their study of literature. They'd gone beyond
understanding, analyzing, and criticizing. They were *doing*.
They had crafted their own literary artifacts. They'd become
authors themselves.

C. H. Knoblauch and Lil Brannon write, "*All* human beings
share in the creative ingenuity which is supremely articulated
by Shakespeare" (1984, 73). The ability to make comes with
being human. But dare students enter the very arena in which
renowned authors have performed? Certainly. Besides, it's
inevitable. When students write, they enter a kinship with
the authors of all the ages, sharing with them a common and
noble intent.

"Ah, yes," I hear a voice saying, "but there is a substantial
difference in quality between a modern teenager's trifling ditty
about rock music and literature that has survived for 400
years."

Of course there is, but such a distinction misses the point.
The genius and deep sensibility required to produce writing
of indisputable and lasting quality are not what most writers,
be they students or adults, share with Shakespeare. No, they
share something universal and more elemental. They share
the need and ability to create. With words on paper Shakespeare
strove to make personal meanings clear, to move audiences
in some way. When students write, they engage in precisely
the same act.

I've never met an English teacher who didn't want students
to appreciate great literature and writers. To achieve this we

must link students with the greats who have written. And we can do that by letting them engage in that "creative ingenuity."

Assignments like "Rock Fantasia" let students make literature from the secure base of a model. In fact, David Foster in *A Primer for Writing Teachers* (1983) cites William Gruber's argument that such imitation "can be a way for students to integrate into their own composing the strategies of professional writers" (134). Although I didn't realize it the day I talked myself into the "Rock Fantasia" assignment, the idea of imitating authors' forms or taking off on their subject matter was in my subconscious. A couple of years earlier at the Ohio Writing Project summer institute a fellow teacher introduced me to the idea. She'd had her students imitate the form of William Carlos Williams's "The Red Wheelbarrow." I had my students try that one, too. The results were sensitive, serious, humorous, and sometimes acerbic, as the next poem illustrates:

So much depends
upon
e. e. cummings
with his whimsical verse
beside the Alka-Seltzer

   Greg Taggart, junior

Another poem that lends itself to an imitative assignment is "Chicago," Sandburg's tribute and fine defense of his adopted city. The subject for the students' writing, of course, is not Chicago, but rather the city, town, or village where they live. The poems the students produced in completing this assignment were steeped in their knowledge of the history, lore, and characters of their hometown. Some of these I sent to the editor of the local newspaper, who gladly published them. The assignment went beyond the classroom to awaken community pride, to create positive public relations for the school system, and, most importantly, to promote student writing.

Some of the poems, though, I wouldn't have dared send the newspaper, although I read them to the class. Given our wonderfully pluralistic American society, not all the poems patterned after "Chicago" were tributes and defenses of the home city. Some were virulent indictments and scathing satires.

To read examples of these, you will have to wait until your own students write them.

Imitating the forms of professionals is fun, instructive, and confidence-building. The model usually provides just the right amount of framework to lead students into their own language. But literary imitation is merely one way of creating writing. Certainly, students should go beyond that.

They should be striking out on their own, creating literary artifacts of personal importance, trying just about every genre of literature they study. By the time a year is over students in my classes may have written character profiles, fiction, nonfiction, free verse, haiku, limericks, brief dramas, philosophical arguments, and "occasional" verse. These they create out of their own experience and imaginations. They are writers.

Literature offers readers such a rich store of subject matter that I sometimes ask students to turn their making of literary artifacts upon their reading. With this kind of assignment, they not only practice making a literary genre, they also extend and consolidate their learning of the literature under study.

Drama

Not full-blown plays do I have students write, but rather "dramatic encounters."

Encounters?

Yes. Not mundane meetings or exchanges of banalities. Ask students to create true encounters.

With some kind of tension involved?

Yes.

Who, may I ask, encounters whom?

Anything goes. Time may collapse. Fiction may encounter reality. Genres may mix. After reading *A Death in the Family*, for example, a student might herself encounter James Agee or young Rufus. In the school cafeteria over Tater Tots and pizza the student engages author or character in some pointed conversation about the novel.

Kind of like an interview?

If you like, or it could be less formal than an interview implies. A variation of this assignment has two authors encountering each other.

That often happened in real life.

But more often it didn't, especially if you want to arrange

some provocative meetings. For instance, what would Emily Dickinson and Walt Whitman have said to each other?

I see what you mean. That would reveal students' knowledge and also let them practice logical and imaginative projection.

And the act of throwing two authors together and creating their talk just might lead students to new perceptions or understandings.

I guess students could write dramatic encounters between characters, too.

That would be natural.

I'll bet Macbeth and King Claudius of *Hamlet* would have a great deal to say to each other about guilt and murder and ambition.

Not to mention women.

I can see such character encounters leading to further analysis of literature if you impressed upon students not to settle for banalities.

And the beauty of it is that the analysis evolves through drama, a form students don't often have much experience with.

A dramatic encounter.

Exactly—speech with some underlying or overt tension, just like you'd find in a play.

Prose

Prose forms may include such things as the following:

• Journal entries or monologs written by students, adopting the persona of a major or minor character. They would try hard to speak in the voice, reflect the concerns, and be faithful to the outlook of the character they choose as they write about significant moments or actions.

• A profile or sketch about a literary character, written in a popular magazine style. *The New Yorker, People, Teen,* or *Rolling Stone* are among the possible models, depending upon what you'd like to teach.

• A hard news story, editorial, or feature article about some telling incident in a novel. This could also teach students the strengths and limitations of these various newspaper genres.

• A brief fictional prequel or sequel.

• A letter recommending, censuring, or advising a character.

Songs

Have students write songs—folk, rock, rap, pop, country, or whatever else may appear upon the music scene. Bring in examples, let students spend a day learning the form and structure, then turn them loose creating lyrics about literature.

I've had success letting students write their own blues. Huck Finn Blues, Hemingway Blues, Sonnet Readin' Blues. The blues form is indigenous American music and eminently appropriate for expressing the essence of conflict, dilemmas, and hard times. Plenty of good models have been recorded by B. B. King, Muddy Waters, Lightnin' Hopkins, Eddie "Cleanhead" Vinson, and many others. The assignment is pure fun and an excellent opportunity for students to team up with a partner or two and experience the give-and-take and creative spurring of collaboration.

Poetry

Students may write poems about the theme, characters, or plot of a literary selection. I've found that, given the constraints of the form, students often condense and sharpen their critical comments. You may prescribe a poetic form for students to try—imagist, free-verse, narrative, dramatic monolog, you name it. Or you may have students choose their own. When I asked students to write poems about *The Scarlet Letter*, one girl chose the limerick to assess the characters in a nutshell:

> There once was an imp, name of Pearl
> Who was an illegitamitely conceived, type of girl
> The A made of scarlet
> Revealed her mother a harlot
> However, her father, the priest was the real
> squirrel.
>
> *Kathy Wilham, junior*

When my students create their own literary artifacts, whether to make personal meanings or to respond to literature through them, my idea is to celebrate their creative ingenuity, to let them learn about various styles and genres from the firsthand experience of making them. I want students to reaffirm their elemental kinship with professional writers, those who view writing not as an ordeal that reveals ineptitude, but as an opportunity to create visions.

I seek to narrow the gap that students see between themselves and published authors. I want my high-school students to be more like the first graders I observed in Patricia McLure's classroom at Mast Way School. On their sure, individual roads to attaining full literacy, these children read a wide range of literature, from nonfiction to fantasies; and every morning, before McLure ever said a word to the class as a group, they pulled out their writing folders and began to write. They acted like professionals.

University of New Hampshire literacy researcher Ruth Hubbard reported numerous instances of McLure's students asking questions not only about the writing of their peers, but also about the writing in the trade books they were reading. The first graders were becoming practical critics and confident creators. Because the children were writers, the work of professionals did not intimidate them. They criticized plot movement and characters. They uttered opinions and backed them up. If the ending of a book was in some way dissatisfying, they readily suggested a new one.

I want high-school students to treat literature that brashly, that actively, that intellectually. They can do it if they feel worthy and secure. My responsibility is to see that all my students are enfranchised in the high-school literature class. Their voices count, every bit as much as Updike's and Cather's and Dickens's. So I ask students to make literature for its own sake, and I respect their accomplishments. I've no illusion that I will discover an Emily or Ernest in every classroom. I do believe, however, that every year in each of my classes I will be surprised again and again by the competence, originality, and high quality of literature my students produce.

TO CONNECT PERSONALLY WITH
THEMES AND SUBJECTS

Before we read, I sometimes have students use nonstop, focused writing for five or ten minutes to explore the topic or theme of an upcoming piece of literature. I want them to activate what they already know, for they know much. Through such writing in the past my students have described what they consider the major dilemma faced by modern teenagers. They have explained how they feel when they're compelled to do something. They have revealed their knowledge of American Plains Indians, racial prejudice, and the Great Depression. They have defined adulthood. They have written what they know firsthand of loyalty, suffering, and courage. Name the theme—chances are your students already know a lot about it, have connected with it in highly individual ways, and can summon that connection if given a chance to think powerfully in writing. Before reading of young Sarty's inner turmoil and courageous decision in Faulkner's short story "Barn Burning," one of my students wrote this:

> The little boy was walking around in the store alone. I would say he was about 5 or 6 he walked up to a lady and I couldn't hear what he said. The lady didn't listen—she was old she probably had trouble hearing.
>
> The little boy came right up to me then and said he couldn't find his mom. I took him to the service desk and they described him over the speaker—while he stood there quietly and dry-eyed.
>
> I waited a few minutes and no one ever came to get him. He didn't say anything and he seemed very calm. I decided I better go & get the things I needed so I did.
>
> On my way out I noticed he was still there and I felt bad. I asked them what they were going to do and they told me they had called the police department. An officer was walking in the door then and up to the boy.
>
> The boy was not afraid of the man and answered all his questions promptly. The boy went with the officer and never looked back.
>
> I was thinking that other children would probably be crying their eyes out but this little boy must have been brave. I never found out what happened to him.

Such quick, spontaneous writing enables students to make personal connections with an upcoming reading. They discover that this isn't alien territory they're moving into. This is literature, and literature is life. Students are living the very stuff that literature is made from. When they realize this, their interest heightens.

TO REVEAL FIRST IMPRESSIONS

Literature is intimate and singularly human. It is made by humans, preserved by humans, used by humans. Readers hold literature in their hands. They invest hours of precious time with it. Like writers who have created meaning with words, readers, too, take words and create meaning. Without humans who read, who animate inanimate words, literature would be dormant, an act of creation no longer useful.

Literature is meant for humanity; humanity is diverse. And because the process of reading is creative and idiosyncratic, literature is an open invitation for revealing spontaneous impressions, individual human responses. A dull class indeed is the one in which only the teacher reveals a response to literature. In fact, shared student responses are essential to keep a literature class invigorating, for often teachers have lost the capacity to respond freshly, they have taught a piece so frequently. The possibility exists for students to bring all they know, all they are, and all they have been to understanding and experiencing literature. Writing offers a way for both students and teachers to make that response, that thinking, intense and concentrated.

Nancie Atwell elicits her eighth graders' honest responses by asking them to write letters to her and their classmates about the books they are reading (1986, 138). In the course of a year, her students write thousands of letters. Taking Nancie's lead, I have had my students, too, write letters about literature. In a missive to Anna, Karen, a junior, wrote,

I'm reading *The Heart Is A Lonely Hunter*, by Carson McCullers. It is really a good book. You really get to know the main characters in the book well. Each chapter is about a different one of the main characters. You can really relate to these people because they are so real. The girl in here, Mick, reminds me of myself when I was younger, because she is such a tomboy. I think that the book is trying to show how people are hunting for love and "different ways" people do it. The main characters are easy to remember because there isn't a whole lot of them. The book is really interesting once you get into it. It is hard to believe how much a deaf mute can do in soceity, as one of the main characters is a deaf mute. At points in the book you can feel like your a character in the book to.

Friends Always,

Karen Braley

There is chit-chat here, much routine information about the book. But some of her first impressions indicate that Karen has learned something specific from her reading, has responded emotionally and intellectually to the literature. She has made assertions:

I think that the book is trying to show how people are hunting for love and the "different ways" people do it.

It is hard to believe how much a deaf mute can do in soceity. . . .

At points in the book you can feel like your a character in the book to.

Karen did not elaborate on these points in her letter, but the assertions obviously have stories behind them. She knows particulars that can back them up. Any one could lead to an in-depth discussion or become the focus of a paper. An important thing to remember is that Karen raised these points in a letter to a friend, an informal, yet purposeful piece of writing.

TO UNCOVER READING-THINKING PROCESSES

I want my students to think as deeply as they can about their reading. And although I want to share my thoughts about literature, I'd like the students themselves to generate many of the ideas they think about and discuss. This is one way they become better readers—by uttering their puzzlements about the reading, articulating problems, and pushing forward language to explain or explore those puzzlements and problems.

Gary Lindberg, professor of literature at the University of New Hampshire, urges English teachers to address a far more important skill than merely passing on to students so-called correct readings of literary texts. "Instead of leading them to right readings of books or proper historical and critical placement of them," writes Lindberg, "the teacher helps students get into new relations with words on the page. We don't give them truth; we give them power. Or more precisely, we help them seize on their own authority as interpreters" (1986, 154).

We want students to interact with literature, to make their meanings, not merely receive them. To this end I sometimes have my students write the story, or narrative, of their reading (Elbow 1985). I ask them to use written language to uncover their mental processes of reading, their changes in thinking, their developing awareness, and their emerging understanding. No more do I have students look at questions that follow an anthologized piece of literature. Instead, I spur them to ask their own questions and venture their own answers, as Lucy Calkins recommends (1986). In the out-of-school world of reading, no questions follow the text (238).

On one occasion my sophomores read "Gaston," William Saroyan's sparely written short story of artistic sensibility, differing values, and parental influence. I gave students the time they needed to write the story of their reading.

A tenth-grade boy wrote:

> This story is probably the first story I've read out of this book that I fully understand. Its about a little girl thats staying with her father that she hardly ever gets to see, it took me a while to find out that her mother and father were divorced. He buys some peaches while they were walking in the nieghborhood. When they bring them home and start eating them, the father finds a worm in his peach. The little girl asks, "who is it." And her father gives it a name, like he was a long lost friend. After a while she wants a peach with somebody living in it. so her father goes out and buys her a bad peach. While he's gone her mother calls to tell her about a birthday party. When the father gets back she doesn't want the peach anymore because she thinks its ugh. When she leaves they just shake hands as if they were strangers.

Although this student has neither asked questions nor conjectured about the decisions and actions of the characters, he has pinned down some literal facts of the story that have further interpretive significance. Why does the father give the worm (actually a bug) the name Gaston as though it were some "long lost friend"? Why does the girl change her mind about Gaston after the telephone conversation with her mother? In the final line, the writer recalls Saroyan's simile ("as if they were strangers") to describe the handshake between father and daughter. How did they arrive at that juncture in their relationship? This writer is moving in the right direction. I'd like to see him travel further and risk speculations about the significance of the facts he knows. He will do that if he hears his classmates speculate and I keep urging him to practice drawing conclusions.

Another boy in the same class interacted with "Gaston" this way:

> When I read this, I was wondering why they were just eating peaches? Are they poor or is it a snack. Why did the girl say that the man would have been a total stranger if he wasn't her father? It sounded to me that she had doubts about him really being her father. Why did her father get the peach that was flawed? I think he ate it so it wouldn't go to waste or so she wouldn't find anything in it. Why did they call the bug Gaston. I think it might mean bug or something in French. Why didn't the man squash the bug? Maybe he felt responsible for it loosing its home. Why wasn't the mother living with the father? They must have gotten divorced. Was the mother rich? She must have been, because she sent the chauffeur after the girl. I want to know why the girl squashed the bug anyway? I think she squashed it because of her mother when she talked to her it brought the high styled living out in her. Why didn't he hug her when she left. Were they trying to hide that he was her father. Why did the man feel like Gaston? He probably felt like Gaston, because he didn't feel like he had a home without his daughter.

This writer took to extremes my encouragement to ask questions, firing a barrage of them. That alone, I think, is a step toward deeper involvement with reading. This writer didn't stop at questions, though. He let them lead him to real interaction with the story by venturing answers. The writing-thinking caused him to wonder about three important facts: why the father didn't squash Gaston; why his daughter did; and why, at the end of the story, the father felt like Gaston.

The writing caused all the students to think more deeply. Our ensuing class discussion was brief and spirited. We started with a couple of students reading their writing aloud. From there, other students added comments and explained their varied responses and interpretations. Sometimes both the students and I revealed misreadings of the text. I sought an atmosphere in which those errors of comprehension would not embarrass individuals, that instead they would inform the group members of reading processes, of how we must all work for meaning.

"Reading is messier than we like to believe," writes Lindberg (154). I want my students to understand this as they interact with literature. Neat answers to meaning often exist only in teacher's manuals, which is the reason I don't use them. I want to approach literature honestly, on my own merits, just as I ask my students to.

The literary discussions offered in teacher's manuals have too often made a fraud of me. With them, I have conducted discussions with loaded dice. That made students the gamblers, not me. And they usually lost—unless they were lucky enough to beat enormous odds and come up with the ideas and textual nuances I had in my head. With someone else's published, authoritative interpretations leading my thinking, I rarely took seriously students' interpretations and never resisted the English-teacherly impulse to promote a single right reading, to give truth, to tell students what to think.

But students interacting with literature—and, to my mind, that means often writing about it—need not listen to a teacher tell them what to think. *They* think. Better to have students gather in small groups with their writing, share the stories of their reading—the questions, the misreadings, the insights—and discuss the possibilities and revelations uncovered. The discoveries will be human, surprising, often astute. And after such sharing, a large group discussion is in order, indeed, much to be desired, to find out what everybody thought, including the teacher—another honest reader in the classroom.

Through literature our students can learn more about the process of reading. And they can also learn more about the process of writing. We know that professional writers are also wide readers. And we know that alert readers frequently learn things about writing from their reading. I have pushed students to explore this relationship between reading and writing, asking them to write and uncover what they are learning about writing from the books they are reading. In separate classes, two juniors wrote about a similar aspect of the same novel, but from different perspectives. Because we shared their observations in class, the responses led to some good talk about reader expectations, voices and form in fiction, and so-called rules of composition.

Janet wrote, "I guess what my book taught me is to be open minded about books written in different ways. Like the way *The Color Purple* is written in letters and also in Negro dialect."

And Patty: "Alice Walker showed me that you could break every rule of writing I learned in tenth grade and write one of the best books ever."

REFERENCES

Agee, James. 1967. *A Death in the Family*. New York: Bantam Books. (Originally published in 1957 by McDowell, Obolensky, NY.)

Atwell, Nancie. 1986. "Making Time." In *To Compose: Teaching Writing in the High School*, edited by Thomas Newkirk. Portsmouth, NH: Heinemann, 1986. (Originally published in 1985 by the Northeast Regional Exchange, Inc., Chelmsford, MA.)

Calkins, Lucy McCormick. 1986. *The Art of Teaching Writing*. Portsmouth, NH: Heinemann.

Elbow, Peter. 1985. Talk given at the 1985 National Council of Teachers of English Fall Convention, Philadelphia, PA.

Faulkner, William. 1974. "Barn Burning." In *Look Back in Love*, edited by Sara Rosner. New York: Scholastic Book Services. (Originally published in *Harper's Magazine*, June, 1939.)

Foster, David. 1983. *A Primer for Writing Teachers*. Upper Montclair, NJ: Boynton/Cook.

Hawthorne, Nathaniel. 1965. *The Scarlet Letter*. New York: Bantam Books. (Originally published in 1850.)

Knoblauch, C. H., and Brannon, Lil. 1984. *Rhetorical Traditions and the Teaching of Writing*. Upper Montclair, NJ: Boynton/Cook.

Lindberg, Gary. 1986. "Coming to Words: Writing as Process and the Reading of Literature." In *Only Connect: Uniting Reading and Writing*, edited by Thomas Newkirk. Upper Montclair, NJ: Boynton/Cook.

McCullers, Carson. 1953. *The Heart Is a Lonely Hunter*. New York: Bantam Books. (Originally published by Houghton Mifflin, 1940.)

Salinger, J. D. 1964. *The Catcher in the Rye*. New York: Bantam Books. (Originally published by Little, Brown and Co., 1951.)

Sandburg, Carl. 1950. "Chicago." In *Complete Poems*. New York: Harcourt, Brace and Co. (First collected in *Chicago Poems*, 1916.)

———. 1950. "Jazz Fantasia." In *Complete Poems*. New York: Harcourt, Brace and Co. (First collected in *Smoke and Steel*, 1920.)

Saroyan, William. 1984. "Gaston." In *Literature, Blue Level*, edited by David W. Foote and Brenda Pierce Perkins. Evanston, IL: McDougal, Littel & Co. (Originally published in *The Atlantic Monthly*, 1962.)

Walker, Alice. 1982. *The Color Purple*. New York: Harcourt Brace Jovanovich.

Williams, William Carlos. 1966. "The Red Wheelbarrow." In *The Literature of the United States*, Vol. 2, 3d ed., edited by Walter Blair et al. Glenview, IL: Scott, Foresman and Co. (Also found in *The Collected Earlier Poems*. NY: New Directions Book, 1938, 1951.)

10

Writing Amid Literature
Part Two: Restoring a Reputation

Writing critical essays belongs in the literature class. But before I write further, I must distinguish between two kinds of essays I've read over the years. One kind is richly textured, highly individual, eminently readable; the other is mechanical, impersonal, and decidedly unreadable. Too many students learn to produce the latter. And too many English teachers, guided by myths of composition and a skewed notion about the kind of writing college teachers will demand, end up teaching their students to write stiff, laborious, pseudo-objective, nobody essays.

There's a kind of thinking in many of our secondary schools that divides writing into two distinct categories: creative and expository. Creative writing has its small niche for those artsy types, the thinking goes, but it falls far short of meeting the rigorous demands of the writing that must be done for education, business, and government—expository writing.

Through years of pedantic prescription, expository writing has developed identifiable characteristics. It frequently employs an elevated, thesaurusized vocabulary. Its pacing is even, tightly regulated, moderate. Humor and lightness are denied entry, although the tone is often so serious, so lofty, it becomes laughable. All flash, color, and surprise are quelled. Figurative language—a sure sign of frivolity and imprecision—is barred. In short, the thinking that has severed writing into the mutually exclusive categories of creative and expository is responsible for the production of a great deal of bad writing, especially in the realm of the essay.

A friend of mine, Don Daiker of Miami University in Oxford, Ohio, has for three years now judged writing submitted by high-school juniors for the NCTE Achievement Awards in Writing. Few in number, these students represent a kind of cream, having been recognized in one way or another as excellent writers by their home schools. The students submit a sample of their best work and also write an impromptu essay within a seventy-five-minute time limit on one of two topics provided by NCTE.

The impromptu essays, reports Daiker, "*all* sounded alike: each was dull, obvious, voiceless, and vague. . . . Interestingly, there was not a great deal more variety on papers submitted as a sample of the candidate's best work: they too lacked originality and passion" (pers. com., 1986).

The pieces had one further thing in common, Daiker noted: Each was nearly perfect in grammar, usage, punctuation, and spelling. But correct use of semicolons could not compensate for the lack of inventiveness; orthographic flawlessness could not hide a dearth of specific detail; agreement of subjects and verbs could not resuscitate dead sentences. The writing remained lifeless—no vigor, no voice, no pulse.

Expository writing need not be written this way. The essay does not have to induce yawns and drooping eyelids. In a sensible piece titled "On Essaying," James Moffett points out that we have essays in the English language that rival poetry for "color, depth, and stylistic originality" (1983, 171).

Our best essays are not written in depersonalized prose that feigns an air of objectivity and impartiality, that never slips into narrative, description, or dialog. No, the real tradition of the essay is "a candid blend of personal and universal" (171). In essays as well as other genres, we want chords struck that touch our humanity, viewpoints that sing individuality. "What we really want to help youngsters learn," writes Moffett, "is how to express ideas of universal value in a personal voice" (170–71).

When students write essays in my classes, I urge them to discover personal links with the literature and to let that guide them in choosing the topic and focus of their papers. I help them learn to do this by demonstrating through my own writing and storytelling how I have made personal links with literature. To enable students to make meaningful and fruitful topic choices, I use class time to let them confer with each other and with me about their ideas.

In one batch of twenty-five essays, David, a junior, demonstrated to me and his classmates that a literary essay could be simultaneously personal, universal, critical, interesting, and readable.

I HATE CATS

Driving down my street one day I noticed a red and white pile of fur. As I got closer I noticed it was a cat that had been caught by the front wheel of my neighbor's car. I stopped and went up to look at it. It was still alive. No one was home so I scraped the cat up and wrapped it in a towel to get him to the vet. When I got there the cat was dead and I felt it was my fault. I hate cats, but at that time I would have done anything—even get blood in my car—for that flat cat.

—Sympathy.

This is how Dalton Trumbo gets his view on war across in *Johnny Got His Gun*.

> *He was quiet just like a storekeeper taking spring inventory and saying to himself I see I have no eyes better put that down in the order book. He had no legs and no arms and no eyes and no ears and no mouth and no tongue.*
> (page 62)

Meet Joe Bonham, Trumbo's lead character. Anybody that saw someone in Joe's condition would either be immediately sympathetic or turned-off by what he had to say. To avoid the latter Trumbo gets the reader to relate to Joe by telling "prewar" stories. This gets the reader to say, "Hey, I know what this guy felt like here. The same thing happened to me once!" Then, after more thought the reader says, "What if it was me in this condition? I'd want people to listen to what I had to say." Then, without knowing it, the reader lets Trumbo plant his thoughts in his head.

". . . *My father just died.*" (page 4) This is what Joe tells his foreman. Everyone has lost a family member. We can all sympathize with the way he felt.

As a little kid I remember having friends come over and we would dress up in my dad's clothes to feel grown-up. Well, here is a quote from page 20 that tells how Joe felt after receiving a pair of socks: *"The socks seemed to mean a step forward into a grown-up future."*

I feel sorry for anyone that loses a girlfriend. What makes it worse is Joe loses his girl to his best friend Bill Harper. Ouch. *"Diane was there on the front steps with her arms around somebody . . . They were kissing . . . It was Bill Harper."* (page 52)

Of all the things that have happened to me in life the worst I've ever felt was when I wrecked my dad's car. Not just any car. HIS car. His 1967 Chevy Malibu. No rust. Left to him by his father with only 37,000 miles on it.

> *He thought about the rod* (car) *again and then he knew why his father was a failure. It wasn't that his father didn't provide for his family and keep them in clothes and food and pleasure. It was all very plain now. His father didn't have enough money to buy another rod* (car). *Even though the rod* (car) *was his father's most cherished possession now that it was gone he wouldn't have enough money to buy another and he was a failure.* (page 107)

That's where I fell into Trumbo's trap. Throughout the rest of the novel I paid total attention to everything Joe thought. Even though I found out later I disagreed, at the time I believed what he said out of sympathy.

Once the reader relates to Joe, Trumbo's job is over. Emotions take over and this is what allows Trumbo to get the reader to take his point of view.

David Van Cleave, junior

David wrote his fine essay over a period of five days. After finishing the novel, he'd had plenty of time to plumb the depths of his thought and emotion, choose his own topic, write a draft, try it out on his peers, and craft the final product.

But most of the essays written in high-school literature classes are not papers that have been carried through an extended writing process. Most are of the test variety, to be completed within a set time limit. I use essays for testing, too. In literature classes they are so much more suitable than objective tests.

At their best, essay tests ask students to call upon their learning, personally connect with it, discover new thinking both before and during their writing, synthesize all of that, and communicate it powerfully.

At their worst, essay testing tyrannizes students, sends them distorted messages about writing, and reduces the creation of an essay to a perfunctory, rapid-fire task, void of surprise, delight, and discovery.

And that's why I am cautious about how I write and use essay prompts. Conceived too narrowly, answered in an anxiety-ridden atmosphere, essay tests can abuse students and perpetuate harmful myths about how writing is created.

When I took the mandatory freshman English course in college, one bold classmate asked our teacher, a harried doctoral student, if our in-class, fifty-minute essays would be evaluated by the same criteria as our out-of-class essays. The teacher's nervous, preoccupied expression turned to astonishment. "Certainly," he said.

I felt uneasy about his answer, but hunched up in my seat like a dogged Hemingway hero and thought, "Well, Tom, this is college, the big leagues, and an English major must deal with such things."

But the unease stayed with me, and now, these many years later, I decry the teacher's attitude. I object because I am acutely aware of the differences in clarity of expression, intellectual depth, and effectiveness of language between my own first and final drafts. Were I unable to revise my initial writing, written composition would hold little joy for me. My writing is strengthened by the additions, deletions, and transformations that occur as I interact with drafts. I need revision time to explore, create, and refine my thinking, to expand, clarify, and polish my writing. First drafts—what I produce during essay tests—are no true measure of my writing or my thinking.

A writing diet heavy in timed essays can also undermine the teaching of writing. The constant call for immediate performance creates damaging misconceptions about written composition. Students come to see writing as a task to be done hastily. They see that, aside from correcting a few spelling or punctuation errors, not much can be gained from a second look at what they've written. Indeed, even if a second look enabled them to see where significant changes needed to be made in the text, there is little time to make them. And they learn that always, always, following the production of writing comes a judging that will not so much celebrate their successes as it will expose their inadequacies.

In most cases, answering an essay prompt is a pressurized, one-shot affair. And as an English teacher I recognize that our students must learn that on occasion they must produce for certain audiences "single-draft, final copy," as my friend Carolyn Smith calls such writing. They'll have one chance to do it. No looking back. Students may some day sit in an office and write paragraphs on job applications; they may compose descriptions of auto accidents written in the backseats of police cars; they may write letters to friends and notes to the ones they love. But we must keep in mind that although these impromptu writing situations exist, they are the exceptions, not the norms of written composition.

Whether self-imposed or outwardly imposed, most writing tasks allow time for reseeing and polishing. Therefore, I explain to students the special circumstances of in-class essay writing, how it differs from other writing opportunities, what they will be called upon to attempt. Furthermore, I read the prose produced under such constraints with a more compassionate eye.

Essay tests may be damaging in yet another way—*if* students are asked to do no more than merely reproduce in some standard form information and ideas that have been given to them. When essay prompts are this meager in scope, classrooms become factories, students the assembly-line laborers, teachers the supervisors in charge of quality control. Students all seek to produce the same essay product; teachers gauge the work against a notion of perfection they have in their heads.

Such essay prompts trivialize writing, notes Donald Murray, requiring "students to deliver *our* messages from *their* mouths, and correcting anything that surprises us" (1985, 88).

To devise good essay prompts, those that neither trivialize writing nor undermine a sound perception of how writing is usually produced, we must begin by acknowledging that students can create meanings that have never occurred to their teachers. And we must reaffirm our belief in the incredible generative power of language. Writing can do so much more than the menial job of showing teachers that their students have memorized certain facts and can fit them into an arbitrary, often stultifying rhetorical form.

Unwelcome in my classroom are essay prompts like these:

> Discuss the eight tenets of Transcendentalism and their influence upon American literature.

or

> Describe Henry David Thoreau's character traits and personality. Use the content and style of *Walden* to support your assertions.

Surely students must learn the invaluable skill of discussing and synthesizing ideas and diverse bits of information. These essay prompts do ask students to synthesize to some extent, although the first might easily be reduced to little more than listing. My major objection to them is the pat answer they expect. Eight tenets—no more, no less. In addition, neither prompt leaves students much room to connect personally with the information they are asked to write about, a crucial factor for teenagers learning to create effective expository writing.

A good essay prompt, then, does not just ask students to synthesize and communicate. It invites them to push forward their own thinking. It offers a chance to connect personally with concepts under study. It solicits their voices and imaginations.

The following prompt is an example of what I mean. To show what I further learned after the students wrote, I reprint the prompt exactly as I first composed it:

> Essay question. (5 points for solid thesis statement; 35 points for the body.)
>
> Through the miraculous, self-reliant power of Romano, Henry David Thoreau (same character, personality, and principles) has been transported to the present. And, lo and behold! He is seventeen years old.
>
> Write an essay in which you describe seven of his possessions that reflect his personality, character, and concerns. Explain what each possession reveals about him.

In the body of your essay be expansive, imaginative, and thoughtful. I am looking for you to make connections that will surprise, delight, and inform me.

I was pleased with this idea, which came to me as I drove home from school over hilly countryside. But even so, the words of my essay prompt reveal the fastidious teacher in me fretting about evaluation. Seven possessions; thirty-five points for the body. That makes each mention of a possession worth five points, depending, of course, upon how well the student convinces me that the item mentioned reveals something valid about Thoreau. The student might end up with 4.6 points or 3.95 points or 2.775 points—you never know. Good grief!

Those mathematical safeguards proved unnecessary. Soon after I began reading the essays, I became embarrassed by my reductionist need to quantify the depth and range of my students' freewheeling thinking, to measure in millimeters human feats of imagination and synthesis. I'd asked the students to surprise, delight, and inform. That they had—so well, in fact, that I threw out the point formula, grouped the essays holistically into four or five stacks, then evaluated each with a sharp eye to individual accomplishment. Grades were high. My students demonstrated significant personal understandings of Thoreau. Beyond that (and this is what made the essays so surprisingly fun to read), the choices for Thoreau's possessions revealed the splendid diversity and individuality of those teenagers.

THOREAU AT 17

Henry David Thoreau has come back to life and he is living here in rural Ohio. Since possessions say a lot about a person, the following is a description of seven of Dave's things.

He has a journal with him. He always writes notes and stuff in it. I've heard he has more than twelve volumes at home.

Another thing is his books. He doesn't read Harlequin or sports stories but Vonnegut Salinger and Jack London. You know, the really challenging stuff. That's all I see him with. He only reads things that are thought provoking.

He's a really simple guy. His clothes are all faded or patched or both. It doesn't look like he combs his hair. His shirts are not tucked in and his tennis shoes have holes in them. He never wears fashionable things, just jeans and a shirt.

He has a dog that he takes with him any where he goes. It's a beagle named Ralph. He (Dave) really likes nature and animals. He's always outside sitting in the sun or reading a book.

His car is an old beat-up Ford. He only uses it to drive to work. The other places he walks to. He works in a place where they make tooth brushes. It's not a very nice place but it pays for his needs.

He has a stereo and a few records but he doesn't listen to it much. He hasn't much reason to. He never goes to concerts even parties. He just communes with nature or reads.

Last of all is his movie camera. He makes little films of birds and stuff; whatever he's interested in. He got some great shots of a deer because he sat so still for a long time. He really understands nature.

Ken Ballinger, senior

Our essay prompts should not merely be exercises in writing to a particular form, in revealing limited information learned specifically for a test. They should instead be opportunities for our students to create additional original thinking about literature. And while essay prompts will also give students experience at producing first-draft final copy, we teachers would do well to keep in mind the origin of *essay*, a word derived from the French term *essai*, which means "to attempt" (Moffett 1983, 171).

Often, the heavy emphasis in essay evaluation is on the clear, persuasive communication of ideas—a power that every teacher wants students to develop. But that power of writing must be balanced with another—one not as generally acknowledged, but equally important; one whose method is not calculated, but is, rather, spontaneous, intuitive, even mystical. Those who write, who listen intently to their inner voice and follow it faithfully, possess a power unsurpassed for stirring the subconscious, for linking new knowledge with old, for making the unknown known. Our essay invitations should allow students to cultivate both powers of writing: to communicate and to discover. Composing such invitations isn't easy, but is imperative for teachers to strive for.

What we want to do is leave doors ajar for students so they can push them open, explore the other side, and reveal their discoveries. The Thoreau prompt enabled my students to do that. Some weeks later, when we studied another nineteenth-century American writer, I discovered that sometimes a nontraditional writing invitation calling for nontraditional writing might leave an alternate door ajar, one that students never would have considered passing through.

I had been desperate trying to devise a suitable essay prompt for Walt Whitman, whom my students saw as vastly different from anyone we'd read, including Thoreau. An Ohio Writing Project friend of mine, Pam Emnett of Portsmouth, Ohio, suggested that I have each student write her own "Song of Myself." I loved the idea. It seemed the perfect assignment for Whitman. When I began to write, however, so imbued was I with Whitman's voice and spirit that I couldn't write a traditional essay prompt. Instead, I wrote this:

ESSAY TEST (OF SORTS)

You read Whitman's "barbaric Yawp,"
his "Song of Myself."
In s p r a w l i n g
                    BOLD
                                    free
                                            verse
he
proclaimed his individuality
announced his unconventional philosophies
recreated empathetic scenes with striking,
vivid detail
                    (hounded slave and stallion so fine)
spoke the rude truth
shot his vision of life over the roofs of the world

and a real man emerged!

Now—here's what you must do
for the writing part of the test: Sing

the song of yourself.
Mimic the Whitman form,
but the subject matter
must spring from
your individuality
your philosophies
your selected scene
your rude truth
your vision of life

Go to it—now is not a time to
lean and loafe at your ease.

"Oh, God," I heard muttered from the first student who turned to the test. Moans and short, anguished cries followed from others. But there was no need for concern. They had merely been caught off guard by encountering such an assignment on this, a "formal" test. Since the students had been reading much Whitman, they soon became comfortable with the style of my prompt, discovered its sense, and began to work.

Furiously, I must add. I let them do so for the next forty minutes. Before the bell rang, I asked them if they needed more time. "Yes," they clamored. "Well," I said, with elaborate reluctance, "all right. Work on them tonight and hand them in tomorrow."

Of course, my essay test of sorts was no essay test at all. Certainly none of my students believed the prompt called for them to write a sentence like "Walt Whitman was a great writer whose style embodied numerous unique elements that exerted a strong influence on poets to come." That was a relief. I felt no pedagogical pangs of remorse. Students run into the kind of writing invitation I gave them rarely enough in test situations.

I did experience pedagogical euphoria, though, for the prompt accomplished several goals I aim for in my classes. The students saw their teacher truly affected by his reading, connecting personally with it. They saw him respond to that reading with writing. The style of my prompt required them to read in the same way they had been reading Whitman. It invited them to cut loose, look deep, and discover. It asked them to communicate. And the extra time I offered permitted them to revise.

Evaluating their songs of self was a pleasure. I couldn't wait to finish reading one so that I might begin another. The students showed me what they had learned about Whitman's sensibility and style. Of more interest, however, were the individual journeys, both outward and inward, that each student took, much as Whitman himself had. One girl wrote:

I sing the song of myself,
Telling the world who I am,
Showing them the real me.
I am an individual,
I am unique.
There is no one like me,
There will never be anyone as great as I am,
For as long as I live.
I look at a sleeping baby.
His body rolled in a ball,
His tiny hands are clenched fists,
Ready to protect against anything that
might want to harm his new self.
I know how that infant feels.
I have my clenched fists protecting my body
from anything that might want to harm me.
Every day I am like that infant.
When something is wrong,
I let people know about it,
Just as the baby lets out a cry.
Mother comes and feeds the babe when he cries.
Now I seperate myself from him,
from everybody.
I depend on myself for everything,
I can give myself everything it needs to survive.
I see an ant hill, with many ants coming and going.
Their tiny bodies carrying crumbs to their ant
community.
I don't like these ants.
They have to help each other out to live.
I am not like them.
I can take care of myself.
I go to church every Sunday, but find god
hard to understand.

If He is so great, why can't He help the world stop
the wars?
Why do people come to this building,
Worship someone who isn't doing anything
about this world.
Why am I here?
I come to try to understand Him.
Why is He so great?
They say He created the world.
But there are many other worlds than ours.
Did He create them?
Are there other heavenly gods than ours?
I fall into the grass and look up in the sky.
Big, fluffy, white clouds slowly pass by.
What is beyond the clouds?
Are the clouds protecting us from seeing
what is beyond them?
I wish to see what we are being protected from,
I'm not worried, for nothing can destroy myself.
I can handle it.
I am curious, wondering over everything,
learning every day.
Just like the infant.

Tiffany Cadwallader, junior

Every literary creation represents a human triumph. The
study of literature is a celebration of those triumphs and a
promotion of the craft and art of writing. High-school English
classrooms should be full of both the reading and writing of
words, the enjoyment of what has been written and the creation
of what hasn't. Studying literature has the potential to involve
students in all aspects of literacy. It can make them eager to
read; it can make them itch to write. The triumph that comes
with creation wasn't just for Shakespeare. It is for your students.

REFERENCES

Daiker, Don. 1986. Letter to the author, July 2.

Moffett, James. 1983. "On Essaying." In *Fforum: Essays on Theory and Practice in the Teaching of Writing*, edited by Patricia L. Stock. Upper Montclair, NJ: Boynton/Cook.

Murray, Donald M. 1985. *A Writer Teaches Writing*. 2d ed., a complete revision. Boston: Houghton Mifflin Co.

Thoreau, Henry David. 1962. *Walden and Other Writings*. New York: Bantam Books. (*Walden* originally published in 1854.)

Trumbo, Dalton. 1970. *Johnny Got His Gun*. New York: Bantam Books. (Originally published by Lippincott, 1939.)

Whitman, Walt. 1981. "Song of Myself." In *Leaves of Grass*. Franklin Center, PA: The Franklin Library. (Originally published in 1855.)

Literary Warnings

You can become a lost soul in literature just as surely
as you can in any activity where you abandon yourself to
the decisions of others.

William Stafford (1978, 78)

That brilliant professor who taught you modern-Victorian-
Romantic-Shakespearian-critical approaches to literature may
well have been your worst writing teacher. I know I've just
raised your hackles. After all, that brilliant professor provided
the inspiration that propelled you into teaching. Every class
meeting was a tour de force in literary exegesis, a stimulating
hour of one mind succinctly unfolding a critical analysis of
the work under study, weaving together and testing the validity
of years of prominent literary research.

Remember the intricate analysis of the symbolism in *The
Sun Also Rises*? The meticulous explication of every allusion
in "The Waste Land"? The fascinating Freudian interpretation
of *Alice's Adventures in Wonderland*? Remember how raptly
you listened, how fervidly you wrote notes? Remember how
that professor's insights burst in your mind like fireworks,
how he drew everything together so you could begin to truly
appreciate . . . what? Novels? Poetry? Plays? Essays?

No. That brilliant professor of literature taught you to appreciate, uphold, and revere high-grade, premium, hard-to-
come-by, top-of-the-line literary art.

And you did. You did.

But, I repeat, that professor may have been your worst writing teacher.

Speech class—Oral Interpretation. My sophomore year of college. Early in the semester. A student has just finished reading a cutting from Truman Capote's Other Voices, Other Rooms. *The professor and the student trade superlatives about Capote's exquisite prose.*

I know Capote, too, I think. A couple of years earlier a hip high-school teacher had us buy copies of In Cold Blood *just a year or so after it was published. The book had completely engrossed me. I thought it better than James Bond novels. In class we had talked about capital punishment, human psychology, and nonfiction that read like a novel. Yes! (And bless you, Mrs. Hamilton.) I know Truman Capote! And just as I am about to raise my hand. . . .*

"Exactly," says the professor, his facial expression revealing the presence of some foul odor. "Far superior to that potboiler In Cold Blood. *I just don't know what Capote's up to lately."*

The student, a disciple, wears the same repugnant expression as he nods his head sagely.

That brilliant literature professor who may have been your worst writing teacher did not require you to write often. Perhaps you wrote a paper—perhaps. It depended on the class size, how busy he was, how inclined to read student writing. Mainly you wrote essay answers two or three times a semester in which you argued the very theses propounded in class by the professor. If you did write a paper on an undiscussed piece of literature, his critique pooh-poohed your interpretation in favor of those that had been known for years by anyone who knew anything about literature.

But that isn't why the brilliant professor was your worst writing teacher. That's why he was your worst reading teacher.

Later that same sophomore year. Final exam in Oral Interpretation. Each of us must prepare an eight- to ten-minute reading from at least four pieces of thematically related literature.

Some of my classmates are in a quandary. Not me. I know my theme from the outset. Five years earlier my father died senselessly. My mother still hasn't recovered. A girl I love jilted me almost two years ago. I still haven't recovered. Vietnam rages. One of my friends has died there in the fight for Hamburger Hill. John,

Malcolm, Bobby, and Martin have been murdered, and we await the newest political assassination. I'm lonely, afraid, doubting God's existence, and desperate for direction and meaning. Yes, I know my theme. I'm searching for literature that affirms life.

I go to my English Lit professor for advice. I tell Dr. B. about my project, ask him if he has any suggestions.

"What have you chosen thus far?" he asks languidly.

"I found this great poem called 'The Shovel Man' by Carl Sandburg—"

"Sandburg?" he winces. "Must you?"

That brilliant professor of literature may have been your worst writing teacher because he was one of the best of those whose job was to show students how to criticize literature, how to distinguish between good writing and great prose, mediocre writers and great authors. These students would come to know poetry and poets, too. In less time than it takes to scan a line of iambic pentameter, they could tell you whether any given dead poet was bad, good, or sublime.

Mid-May. I've been teaching in high school four or five years. On this Friday evening I am in a checkout line at the supermarket, that cultural melting pot. Summer vacation starts in three weeks. Then I begin taking graduate-school classes again. The local college has just ended the regular academic year.

The fellow in front of me wears a blue sweatshirt, Bermuda shorts, and white canvas shoes. He is slow-moving and benign. The pipe clamped between his teeth has gone out. We inch our carts forward. He begins stacking groceries on the conveyor belt.

"How are you, Professor?" asks the checkout girl.

"Oh, fine," he answers, removing the pipe.

Her eyes dart from item to item; her nimble fingers bang away at the cash register keys. "Enjoying your vacation?" she asks.

"Oh, yes," he says with an ironic laugh. "Immensely. I've begun rereading Proust's Remembrance of Things Past, *just completed volume one."*

"That's nice," says the checkout girl, and then to the bag boy, "Be a sweetie, Marcel, and go get me a price on this pomegranate."

Wide-eyed, earnest, and awed, prospective secondary English teachers often become tainted with snobbery in university

English departments. While studying literature, they gradually don the garb of literary elitists. Peg this writer in a phrase. Sum up this writer in a paragraph. Anyone who knows anything about literature knows who is worth reading and who is not. Eliot is lauded, Sandburg dismissed; James extolled, Steinbeck disdained. The students adopt the attitudes and platitudes of a brilliant professor. They become pseudoscholars of *lit*-tra-chure, zealots whose mission is to promote reverence and right readings of the great traditional literature of England and America—at any cost.

"Wait a minute! These brilliant professors of literature you malign are the keepers of our literary heritage. Their scholarship helps preserve the best that's been written in the English language."

"I know."

"Shakespeare, Faulkner, Chaucer, Dickinson, Yeats, Hawthorne. . . ."

"I know."

"Are you suggesting we shouldn't keep those voices alive, shouldn't perpetuate them?"

"No."

"What then?"

"This: We mustn't let teachers use the genius of literary masters to oppress our student writers. We must not let literary snobbery demean our students' writing at every turn."

Prospective secondary English teachers are technically education majors. But the overriding influence in how they approach language, reading, and writing is vested in the English Department. English-education majors in my undergraduate days (late 1960s and early 1970s) were required to take only one semester's writing class beyond freshman English. The rest of their requirements and most of their electives were loaded with literature courses—filled with great reading, to be sure, from "The Eve of St. Agnes" to *On the Road*. No arguing that.

But the preparation of these prospective secondary-school English teachers was akin to a terribly imbalanced teeter-totter. On one seat were piled all the literature courses, clinging to each other, fighting for a prominent position; on the other end sat the writing course, immobile, up in the air with little chance to get its feet on the ground.

In recent years the imbalance has been lessened some. University English departments have begun taking the teaching of writing seriously, hiring teachers trained to teach writing, teachers who don't look upon the job of teaching composition as second-rate to teaching literature. Prospective English teachers are learning about writing processes, the development of written language, and modern theories of teaching composition.

But what about literature classes?

Unfortunately, many of them still pass on an elitist attitude, sometimes tacitly, sometimes not.

Graduate school—Literature Education class. The professor waxes long on his love of poetry. He reads aloud David McCord, Eve Merriam, X. J. Kennedy. The students delight in the poems. The professor speaks of the aesthetic quality of words, the inherent music of language, the prominent place that poetry should have throughout the school years, not as a mere lesson or unit, but as an integral part of the school language experience.

The students are moved, convinced that poetry doesn't have to be laid open in a belletristic autopsy, but instead can be shared, enjoyed, exalted.

"Yes," says one student, "and we can have students write poetry, too, and take an active, creative role in the school language experience."

"Write poetry?" says the professor, dubiously. "I don't know about that. Surround kids with poetry, yes. Make it part of the very fabric of their lives, yes. But I can't imagine making children write poetry."

The student is steadfast: "I can't imagine teaching English to students all year and not having them write poetry."

"We must remember," says the professor, "that poetry is the most sophisticated genre of writing. It is writing as pure art, employing meter, rhyme, imagery, tone, mood, and precise diction. Most students can never meet the exacting standards of composing real poetry."

"Still," says the student, "I can't imagine not getting students to try their hands at—"

"Well, that's very different," says the professor. "Maybe 'try their hands' at poetry with the understanding that. . . ."

It is easy to love and respect the prose of literary stars, every word glimmering, every idea constant. But secondary-school teachers must also love and respect their students' writing, perhaps ridden with flaws, but also teeming with potential. Teachers aren't likely to learn to recognize, cherish, and nurture that potential if they assume elitist attitudes about writing. If they log hours sitting in the kinds of literature classes in which a Sandburg and a Steinbeck must be called to task for their limitations and berated for their failings instead of praised and appreciated for their contributions, then those becoming teachers may metamorphose into predatory teachers. And the wobbly, newborn prose of their students won't stand a chance.

University English departments have two crucial responsibilities in training students to take positions as secondary-school English teachers (and granted, that's not their only responsibility). Certainly, these teachers-to-be must become good readers with sharp, discerning eyes, well prepared in literature; but they must also know how to work with vulnerable, learning writers from preadolescence to young adulthood. This job might be a little like training soldiers in all the brutal and deadly tricks of combat, yet trying to keep them compassionate at the same time—a difficult balance to strike, but one that university English departments must accomplish.

On one side, they must preserve the great works of English. They must enable students to become discriminating readers—better readers. And surely, brilliant professors should demonstrate, sans dogma, the "how" of their reading processes.

On the other side, they must ever realize that some of their students will one day be charged with the responsibility of helping adolescents learn to write. And that's not a job for literary elitists; that's a job for literary populists.

My American-literature students sit with me in a circle. Our business for the day is to share poems they've written about characters in *The Scarlet Letter*. But this morning I've learned that prominent children's author and *New Yorker* prose stylist E. B. White has died, and I feel the loss.

I tell the students, juniors and seniors, about the famous author's death. Their faces are blank.

"Don't you know E. B. White?" I ask.

No one shows recognition.

"I'll bet you've all read something by him but have just forgotten his name. For one, he wrote *Charlotte's Web*."

"Oh! E. B. White."

"He wrote *Stuart Little*, too!"

"I liked the *Trumpet of the Swan*."

Soon the students are all talking, exchanging their favorite memories from White's children's literature.

"So E. B. White died?"

"Yes."

"How old was he?"

"Eighty-nine."

There is brief quiet.

"God, did I love *Charlotte's Web*!" says one girl. "I must have read it six times and cried every time."

Finally, my most precocious student speaks up—National Merit Scholar, incredibly well-read, reader of insight and depth. One day, I am sure, he himself will write books. "E. B. White also coauthored *The Elements of Style*," he says, "without doubt the finest, most accurate book ever written about writing well. If E. B. White could leave but one book behind and the choice was between the spider-pig saga and *The Elements of Style*, I'd have absolutely no problem making my choice."

Neither would I.

REFERENCES

Carroll, Lewis. 1946. *Alice's Adventures in Wonderland*. New York: Random House. (Originally published in 1865.)

Capote, Truman. 1948. *Other Voices, Other Rooms*. New York: The New American Library.

————. 1965. *In Cold Blood*. New York: The New American Library.

Eliot, T.S. 1968. "The Waste Land." In *The Norton Anthology of English Literature*. Vol. 2, edited by M. H. Abrams et al. New York: W. W. Norton & Co. (Originally published in 1922.)

Hawthorne, Nathaniel. 1965. *The Scarlet Letter*. New York: Bantam Books. (Originally published in 1850.)

Hemingway, Ernest. 1926. *The Sun Also Rises*. New York: Charles Scribner's Sons.

Keats, John. 1968. "The Eve of St. Agnes." In *The Norton Anthology of English Literature*. Vol. 2, edited by M. H. Abrams et al. New York: W. W. Norton & Co. (Originally published in 1820.)

Kerouac, Jack. 1955. *On the Road*. New York: The Viking Press.

Proust, Marcel. 1981. *Remembrance of Things Past*. Vol. 1. Translated by C. K. Scott Moncrieff and Terence Kilmartin. New York: Random House. (*Swann's Way* originally published in 1913. *Within a Budding Grove* originally published in 1919.)

Sandburg, Carl. 1950. "The Shovel Man." In *Complete Poems*. New York: Harcourt, Brace and Co. (First collected in *Chicago Poems*, 1916.)

Stafford, William. 1978. "Whose Tradition?" In *Writing the Australian Crawl: Views on the Writer's Vocation*. Ann Arbor, MI: University of Michigan Press.

Strunk, William, Jr. 1959. *The Elements of Style*. With revisions, an introduction, and a new chapter on writing by E. B. White. New York: The Macmillan Company.

White, E. B. 1945. Pictures by Garth Williams. *Stuart Little*. New York: Harper & Brothers.

————. 1952. Pictures by Garth Williams. *Charlotte's Web*. New York: Harper & Row.

————. 1970. Pictures by Edward Frascino. *The Trumpet of the Swan*. New York: Harper & Row.

A Creative Current

Some of the bright moments in my life have occurred in classrooms. Many students, no doubt (and perhaps a good many teachers), will scoff at such talk. But I must stick by it. In classrooms where openness prevails and students trust enough to speak and write their minds, where everybody is in on what everybody else is doing, creative energy surges forth, becomes almost palpable. Delightful, exciting, provocative things begin happening. Jazz musician Rahsaan Roland Kirk (1973) called them "bright moments."

In a writing class that fosters bright literacy moments, everybody's voice and vision count. Everybody has the same purpose in common: creating with language. No one is alone in such a community, although solitude is available when needed. There is time to write, revise, and begin anew; time to explore, experiment, read, and talk. Ideas and composing strategies circulate through the classroom. And the teacher is part of the circuitry.

In fact, in the beginning, the teacher is the one who flips the switch that enables everyone to draw from the deep, sustaining power of creativity. The teacher encourages reaching out, making human contact, communicating. Students discuss ideas for writing, read each other's drafts, share their perceptions, talk over writing problems, listen to and celebrate final published pieces.

Minds begin to create, thinking and wandering in new realms. Ideas are formulated in most surprising ways as young writers make their own connections. One day early in a semester

class of juniors and seniors the confusing matter of *lie* and
lay arose. I laid a minilesson on the students, and from there
we began discussing verb irregularity. I said that the foreign-
language teachers would probably be relieved if all verbs were
regular, making conjugation a snap.

I told the students of children's natural inclination to inflect
verbs regularly. I had plenty of examples. At the time, my
language-rattling daughter "taked" her medicine, "buyed" ice
cream, and liked it very much when I "readed" to her. In
no time at all, I argued—say, sixty years—it would be natural
to hear, without flinching, a sportscaster say, "In the fourth
quarter the Bengals goed to work, throwed three touchdown
passes, and beated the Forty-Niners by a point."

"In sixty years I'll be seventy-seven," said one of my students,
"and that sentence will still sound wrong to me."

The subject of verb regularity lay dormant and undiscussed
until the final week of class, when senior James Smith wrote
this:

REGULARITY

Once upon a time there ised a little verb who wanted
to be just like any other word—regular. He haved a
hard time though, because all the other words holded a
grudge against him. He thinked about how he could get
his point across. Then he sitted down and writed a letter
to King Noun. All it sayed ised that the verb wanted to
be regular.

Adjective, the Duke of Description, telled the King
not to even write the lowly little working word back,
but the King doed it anyway. He feeled that all his subjects ared important.

He invited the verb over to his palace. They eated together and singed together and haved an all around good
time. Then the verb heared trumpets and seed someone
come in carrying a paper which the King haved drawed
up. The paper sayed that the verb haved complete
regularity.

That night, King Noun holded a festival for the little
verb. The verb weared his best apparel and buyed a new
hat. At the end of the ceremony, the King and the verb
shaked hands. A bouquet of commas comed from the

crowd of sentences down below. The verb catched it and waved back at the crowd.

Then he feeled a buzzing around his body. He becomed light and it feeled like he flied from the kingdom back to his own home across Parentheses River.

He waked up under his covers and looked around. He was still as irregular as ever and the whole episode had only been a dream. He buried his face in his pillow and cried.

James hadn't drawn only upon my playful suggestion. Two weeks before he wrote "Regularity," another student had written and shared with the class a gentle satire in which he turned the entire high school into a kingdom populated by a king, wizard, and various counts, dukes, princesses, and aides. The student, of course, was a mere aide (for the Princess of Spain) who, traveling passless through the kingdom, was warned by Count Chemistry to beware of the Duke of Detention—the assistant principal—who derived fiendish pleasure from imprisoning foolish aides.

James had reaped the benefits of his intellect's interacting with an environment rich in language use, open to sharing, strong in mutual support, safe for risk taking—an environment created by people gathered for a common purpose. I was a crucial part of it, as was each one of James's classmates. The discovery of our own possibilities helped everybody else discover theirs. We sustained each other.

But I must issue a caution: If the sharing and pacing among students devolve into vicious competition, then the creative atmosphere can turn stressful, crippling, and counterproductive. The pressure on students to compete with and beat each other will inhibit creativity, will make risking anything too dangerous. Instead of stretching, young writers will pull in. Instead of venturing from the beaten path, they will wear a rut in it.

I've seen it happen. In the early days of one class, we did plenty of timed, nonstop writings. Some of the students produced satisfying pieces during these unrevised bursts of written language. At the beginning of each class, before we cut loose on another nonstop writing, I shared two or three from the previous day. I was having great fun with the quality of these writings but soon was brought to my senses when two capable writers wrote about their fears of not matching up to the samples I'd read. If two students had expressed their anxiety, I reasoned, then surely others anguished silently.

When I read those two papers, horror flooded my veins and quickened my heartbeat. Impromptu mental dexterity and first-draft performance had insidiously replaced exploration, learning, and growth as the goals of my writing class. And I had been party to their takeover. Without meaning to, I'd set the students at each other in a debilitating game of intellectual one-upmanship. It tied many of them in knots. The class never entirely recovered.

In many content-area disciplines, of course, competition is the norm. And some students are naturally competitive in any situation. I discourage competition as much as possible, try to value the vision and developing language skill of all my students. But sometimes, because of their social and sexual differences, students spur each other to creation in ways I could hardly plan. And this I don't mind at all. In a class dominated by girls, for example, a boy boldly wrote this poem:

SO WHAT?!

Her skin softened by
"Johnson's Baby Oil"
    Plus
Golden hair streaked by
"Sun-in"
    Plus
Dark beautiful skin by
"Sudden tan"
    Plus
Jeans from
"Paris"
    Plus
Silk shirt from
"Sears"
    Plus
Glittering spiked heels from
"Elder-Beerman"
    Divided By
Movie at
"Towne East" and

Dinner at
"Bonanza"
         Equals
Another
Boring
Saturday Night
Date

Lon, senior

One of his female classmates replied:

HERE'S WHAT, BOZO!

What
    have you got
    to complain about?
You
    should be flattered
    that one would go
    to such trouble
    for you.
It was, after all,
    your sex
    which placed
    such emphasis
    on details.
We just went
    along
    doing what
    we could
    to be noticed.
I wonder
    what you'd do
    if your
    fairy princess
    turned into
    a frog?

Terri Blevins, senior

When searching people interact in a classroom, ideas spark and learning occurs in countless ways, some quite practical, some surrealistically imaginative.

The stylistic sentence fragment "A long pause" shows up in a piece by Dwayne. I mention to him that I had observed the same technique used by his classmate Ben a couple of weeks earlier to indicate an awkward moment between two characters. "Yeah," says Dwayne, "I got that from him when he read to the class. You can't make no kinda symbol for a long pause."

Mick, a devoted thespian, writes an absurdist play about a group of green beans that jimmy loose the lid of their cooking-pot prison and effect a clandestine escape from the kitchen. A couple of weeks later Mick's classmate Bill writes a satire of religious quackery turned into big business: A simple Iowa farmer is struck by the revelation that God is a green bean. He founds the Holy Church of Beans, appears each week on television, and becomes a millionaire. As Bill wrote, "Churches sprouted everywhere."

The twists, turns, and trips of imagination that occur when students interact are a constant source of unexpected bright moments. I've even seen a student inspired by a bothersome classmate:

MUSE JEALOUSY

    Ah c'mon!
      She'll come. Just relax and
        wait.
          and wait.
    and wait.
      your mind is too cluttered.
        clean it out.
        Mm-hmm. That's it
        Oh!
        I can see her! She's
          Tiny.
        Crawling up my desk leg.
    Put out my left hand
      Sit right here.
        Yeah.

Ideas flow too quickly out of her to
  write.
Rugged, rude tapping on my shoulder.
"Whaddyawant, Eddie?"
I see her crawl over to Eddie's
  hand, smiling
    slyly
"Never mind," he says,
  "I've got an idea."

Lori Bailey, senior

If high-school students can transmit creative energy, so, too, can their writing teachers. But to do so they must meet and interact with the common purpose of writing and learning. This doesn't happen at monthly teachers' meetings or occasional district in-service days. For the energy to surge and spread, writing teachers must meet regularly and often. In such meetings they talk about writing, reading, and the teaching of literacy. They share ideas, books, articles, and strategies.

And always they write, sometimes bringing a piece with them, sometimes writing during the meeting, all reacquainting themselves with the process of making meaning with language and paper and pen. No matter what they write about—a Kentucky childhood or a new classroom research idea—their voices, thinking, and words will surprise, stimulate, and instruct. A group of trusted peers provides a safe, Godspeed-wishing atmosphere. The group members benignly pace each other, and the pacing can be exhilarating.

I first experienced such a group in 1981 when I attended the Ohio Writing Project's summer institute at Miami University in Oxford, Ohio, a National Writing Project site. I'd been in stimulating college classes before, but never had I experienced a class like this: twenty-three of us—teachers of kindergarten through grade twelve—from dirt-poor rural schools, over-crowded city schools, and well-heeled suburban schools, all with ideas about teaching writing, all eager to share, burning to learn, and ready to write.

The most important tenet of the National Writing Project philosophy is that writing teachers must write. So, in addition to expecting us to write outside of class, the project directors, Mary Fuller and Max Morenberg, provided us with a blessed, contemplative hour for writing at the same time each morning. That never changed. We could count on it, we looked forward to it, we used it.

The NWP's second most important tenet is that teachers learn especially well from other teachers. So the directors provided plenty of time for peer interaction of all kinds. Each day we met in small groups to listen to and discuss each other's writing. Each day we met as a large group to discuss professional readings and talk teaching pedagogy. Each afternoon we participated in workshops conducted by our colleagues that had grown out of their experience and research.

We transmitted energy daily—took it with us into our nights and weekends. And because writing was the business at hand, the energy found outlet in our written language. We wrote poems, essays, descriptions, case histories, research papers, letters, dialogs, reviews, songs, journal entries. . . . The topics we chose to write about, the genres we experimented with, the tacks we took in composing, the directions we traveled in revision—many were spurred, influenced, or guided by the people with whom we created.

But that was a class. That was at a university. The trick is to bring something like that back to the school or district where you teach. During that Ohio Writing Project summer, we read Peter Elbow's *Writing Without Teachers* (1973). Elbow explains how to form and sustain a writing-support group. No classroom. No credit hours. No grades. No assignments. Just a group of people dedicated to writing regularly, sharing that writing, and responding to it honestly.

I wanted to believe that such a group could exist but had never seen anything close to it in action outside a classroom, until I spent a year at the University of New Hampshire. I was part of Donald Graves and Jane Hansen's reading-writing research team at Mast Way School in Lee, New Hampshire, along with Ruth Hubbard, Lorri Neilsen, Ann Marie Stebbins, and videographer Jim Whitney. We had frequent, close contact with four teachers, the librarian, and the principal.

But Graves and Hansen wanted to keep morale high at Mast Way, wanted to share the research with as many staff members as possible. This was an elementary school, after all, that must function cohesively long after the research team had left. Therefore, we researchers occasionally visited and videotaped in many of the teachers' classrooms. In addition,

Graves and Hansen invited all sixteen staff members to join the researchers in a weekly hour-long meeting for the common purpose of writing, reading, and teaching.

Eleven of the Mast Way staff were participating when I joined the group in its second year. The members had had a year of learning to trust each other enough to write and share. Jan Roberts, the third-grade teacher whose classroom I worked in, told me that the building of trust had been a slow and delicate process. But trust had come. By the time I became part of the group, it was an effective entity.

And I'd never seen the like of it. Seventeen people, all believing in the value of the written word enough to make themselves vulnerable, to take their best shot at putting words on paper and then to read those words to peers. They had learned to do this confidently. For they knew that after the sharing of writing would follow support and cheering and help.

Each of us looked forward to reading our own words. You see, we had discovered something. In addition to learning from each other and sharing in the group energy, we took to the idea of having a supportive, knowledgeable audience to write to. The positive things that happened to each of us are the same things that we like to see happen to the students in our classrooms. Self-confidence grew. Sense of purpose sharpened. Understanding and respect for others increased.

Maybe the best news of all about that group was to come. The following year, after the research team had left, after Donald Graves, Jane Hansen, and the other researchers no longer met weekly with that elementary-school staff, the Mast Way group kept meeting. As I sit writing this, they continue to learn, to grow, and to write. They still transmit the energy.

If real change is going to take place in the way writing is taught in schools, it's going to take more than books about writing, summer institutes, seminars, and in-service days. It's going to take the widespread formation of grass-roots writing support groups like the one at Mast Way, where teachers dedicated to promoting literacy meet regularly to talk about writing, to exchange ideas about teaching writing, and, above all, to stir the creative energy within themselves and each other by writing and sharing.

So reach out. You and your colleagues are readers. You have talked about literature, about teaching strategies. There is no reason you cannot become writers, if you aren't already, and begin sharing your work, transmitting the energy, changing the world. One way to start is by simply giving one of your colleagues a piece of your writing—a letter, a news release, a poem, a description, an essay prompt—it doesn't matter what. Just make sure it's real writing, a piece you would genuinely like another human to respond to. Drop your writing in the colleague's mailbox and ask for some response, perhaps about something specific, if you think that will help her respond.

"Bonnie, I'm not sure my directions are clear on this prompt. Would you tell me what they say to you?"

"Would you read this letter, Phyllis, and tell me how you think the school board will react? Do I need to tone it down?"

After the two of you chat about your writing, offer to respond to hers. Let your sincerity show. Now and then pass along a good article, a stirring poem, another piece of your writing. Soon, I think, you'll be sharing writing often, transmitting more energy.

If you meet a stone wall with one person, remain encouraged. Reach out to another. If your colleagues care for language and writing, your good faith and openness will break through eventually, and then the two of you can reach out to others. Some will join you, some will not. The important thing is to remain open, to continue sending the message of acceptance.

At one meeting in that Mast Way group, Millie Woodward, the Chapter One reading teacher in her last year before retirement, read us a piece that had grown out of research she'd done with her students. Her words were sure, her assertions confident, her speculations provocative. The piece was full of the voices of her students who had talked openly about their reading. Millie had learned things through her research and writing. And she was teaching us about those things as she read. We listened to her rich, deep voice and were instructed and moved. As she said the final word, an impressive, respectful silence spread from where she sat. It reached the outer edge of the room, lasted just long enough, and ended when one of her colleagues uttered a compliment.

Millie, always low-key, willing to help, ready to give learners boosts, surprised us by saying, "I was rather pleased with it myself."

The room burst into delighted laughter, everyone happy with Millie's triumph and glad about her gladness with it.

"Well," said Millie, "when you have it right, you just know it."

Indeed. When creative energy is generated in your classroom, in your peer writing-teaching groups, you will know it, too. It is unmistakable. You will feel it and see evidence of it in the good works of your students and colleagues. Minds open. Spirits rise. Voices gain assurance. The animation spreads to every member of the group. The bright moments come again and again. And you'll know you have it right.

REFERENCES

Elbow, Peter. 1973. *Writing Without Teachers*. New York: Oxford University Press.

Kirk, Rahsaan Roland. 1973. *Bright Moments*. New York: Atlantic Recording Corporation.

Index